LET THE
BIG DOG EAT

COMMONSENSE LESSONS, COURSE-TESTED STRATEGIES, and PROFOUND WISDOM to MASTER GOLF

Aaron Brogan

VELO.
press

an imprint of Ulysses Press
PO Box 3440
Berkeley, CA 94703
www.velopress.com

VeloPress is the leading publisher of books on sports for passionate and dedicated athletes around the world. Focused on cycling, triathlon, running, swimming, nutrition/diet, and more, VeloPress books help you achieve your goals and reach the top of your game.

ISBN: 978-1-64604-742-0
Library of Congress Control Number: 2024941659

Printed in the United States
10 9 8 7 6 5 4 3 2 1

Project editor: Kierra Sondereker
Managing editor: Claire Chun
Copy editor: Paula Dragosh
Proofreader: Renee Rutledge
Front cover design: Jake Flaherty Design
Production: Winnie Liu
Artwork from shutterstock.com: dog © Dodoremeo; golf club © Kozachenko
    Maksym; watercolor background © Buzina Svitlana; golf ball © snygggpix

Thanks to my dad for putting a club in my hands, to my mom for driving me to the course, to Chet for caddying, and to Danielle and Gareth for advising me while I wrote this book.

CONTENTS

INTRODUCTION 7

    About Me 8

    Learning Golf.. 10

    Who This Book Is For 11

    Golf Books 13

    Contents.. 16

CHAPTER 1: THE HISTORY OF GOLF.................. 19

    Ancient Times 20

    St Andrews 21

    Old Tom Morris 22

    Golf in the United States 23

    Professional Golf 25

CHAPTER 2: SETTING UP 31

    Setup 34

    Final Note on Setup 47

CHAPTER 3: THE SWING 49

    Moving the Club 51

    Timing.. 69

    The Strike 80

    Spin and Trajectory 87

    Swing Away 101

CHAPTER 4: CLUBS 103

CHAPTER 5: CHIPPING..115

    How to Chip 119

    Chip Shots 123

Sand Shots 129

Difficult Chips 130

CHAPTER 6: PUTTING 133

Holding the Putter 135

Mark and Replace Your Ball 137

How to Putt 141

Putting Weight 143

Reading Greens 145

Final Thoughts on Putting 150

CHAPTER 7: SCORING 153

Avoiding Blowups 156

Second Shot 159

Hunting Birdies 164

CHAPTER 8: PRACTICING 169

Practice Strategies for Novice Golfers 171

Practice Strategies for Intermediate Golfers ... 173

Practice Strategies for Advanced Golfers 178

Scoring Practice 185

CHAPTER 9: PLAYING GOLF 187

The Rules of Golf 187

Unwritten Rules 193

Drinking on the Golf Course 197

Games 200

Equipment 205

CHAPTER 10: THE END 209

ACKNOWLEDGMENTS 215

ABOUT THE AUTHOR 223

INTRODUCTION

FROM BIRTH, MY LIFE HAS BEEN INTERWOVEN WITH GOLF. AS A BABY, I had a plastic club in my hands before I could toddle. I grew up on the golf course. Playing this sport over the years has been a comfort, a distraction, and a torment too.

I share this not to offer a confession but to help you understand this book. I have been close to golf for a long time. I've played competitively. I've played recreationally. I've worked as a greenskeeper. In the words of Joni Mitchell, I've seen this game from both sides now. From up and down. This book will teach you to play golf, but it's not just about learning to play. There's more to golf than getting a ball in a hole.

This book is instructional. Here I provide the knowledge to teach you to teach yourself. I think that's the only way to learn. It's not *just* instructional though. I want to convey something deeper about the game as I know it.

When I was young, I had all the energy to practice for hours, but I was often lost. I just wanted to know what I was supposed to be doing. When I play with novices now, I see the same thing. That's why I wrote this book—to help bridge the gap.

All of this knowledge I've accrued, I gained through a lifetime of study and experimentation, but here I give it to you.[1] This book contains everything you need to know to play golf well.

ABOUT ME

Growing up, my second home was Purpoodock Golf Club in Cape Elizabeth, Maine. My dad was a competitive amateur golfer, and there, on the putting green, was the place he could most reliably be found.[2] Some of the earliest pictures of us together are on the course. It's where my family congregated. We had dinner at the greenside bar and walked out onto the course in the evenings. The sport was in my blood, and everyone knew it.

As I got older, I kept going to that same place. I got a job on the course at sixteen and started working full-time as a greenskeeper. Six days a week I woke before dawn to cut grass and dig holes, in the coastal fog. I cut cups and placed tees. I seeded grass and rolled greens. I learned golf from the soil.

When I wasn't working, I would practice—pounding balls at the range till the blisters on my hands bled through my glove. In the

---

1 For the low low price of $19.95 in paperback.
2 Still is, inshallah.

crepuscular light of summer evenings, I dialed in my approach shots from the fairways. At night, when my teenage mind was racing, I drove to the course and took long walks under the stars. I took a reverential and serious approach to learning golf and studied it closely.

Around that same time, though, I'd go to the course with my friends to drink malt liquor, smoke swisher blunts, and flip golf carts. I swung like John Daly and Happy Gilmore and hit the ball as hard as I could. I hit high-arcing flop shots, often over the green. I snuck onto private courses and sneered invectives at members who challenged me. I recklessly disregarded putting at all times.

This was the other side of my golfing education. For me, running wild in my teens and twenties, this release was always just as much a part of golf as the slow and meditative solitude. Up and down.

Cape Elizabeth is a kind of fancy town, but Purpoodock was just blue-collar enough to (barely) accept me in my delinquent youth and let me do what I wanted.[3] I am still grateful today for that freedom. I needed it.

Eventually I left home and made a life for myself, and as I got older and made money and friends, my opportunities grew. Golf took on a new role in my life as it helped me build relationships. Some of my closest friendships to this day were formed and solidified on courses in Boston and New York. In my twenties the game started taking me places. I played around the country and eventually around the world.

---

3 The police did detain me on the course once, so I suppose acceptance had its limits.

All the while, I studied and practiced the game. I'm in my thirties now, a lawyer living in Manhattan. These days I can't get out on the course much, but I still have these last twenty-something years of knowledge.

LEARNING GOLF

Because I've been lucky enough to make friends who wanted to play golf with me, I've had the privilege of helping many others with their games. Some of them I even taught to play from scratch.

I meet too many people who want to play golf but don't know how or where to start. As Donald Rumsfeld said, they don't know what they don't know.

More than just "not knowing," many people assume the wrong things. It's been too many years of watching novices make wrong-headed assumptions and practice the wrong things, only to actively harm their games. This is where my guidance is most valuable.

Golf is hard. To hit a little ball to a target more than a quarter of a mile away, then get it to drop into a tiny hole, all in fewer than four swings, golfers must harness both power and finesse. The truth is, neophytes can never do this well from the beginning. Charles Barkley is a world-class athlete, but he still embarrasses himself on the golf course. He's just one of many.

I want the game to be as open and accessible to new players as possible. Being out in lush green fields and leisurely passing your day in the company of friends and strangers is such an uncommon blessing. Sharing it seems obvious.

Not to get too woo-woo on you in the introduction, but there is a spiritual depth out there. There is community, self-exploration, and joy in hitting that little ball to the hole far away.

Indeed, all great golf writers have acknowledged the sport's metaphysical quality. There is just something about the picturesque setting of the game, the complex yet fluid swing, and the camaraderie that comes with it.

It's a beautiful, painful sport. It lures us outside and places us in the company of our brothers and sisters. It forces us to face ourselves and grow.

When we play golf and battle the course, we realize ourselves as humans in the tradition of humanity. A part of nature but apart from nature. In the elements but against them.

The value of golf, then, is more than just another hobby. Through the game, we grow as people. Newcomers have much to gain by learning.

WHO THIS BOOK IS FOR

Let the Big Dog Eat is, first, technical. It's a guide for golfers to teach themselves to play better golf. It doesn't target any skill level. If you have never played golf and want to learn, this book is for you. If you're a shitty golfer and don't want to embarrass yourself in front of your father-in-law, this book is for you. If you're a weekend warrior and want to beat the boys on Saturday, pick up this book. If you're already good, this book will help you get better.

Anyone who reads this book and applies its principles will make themselves a better golfer. You'll learn to identify problems in your technique and strategy and approaches to improve. This book will teach you to assess your weaknesses and use empirical tools to target them for improvement. I'll even teach you the secret to stop hitting your ball out of bounds.

More than any drill, this book emphasizes a methodology to refine and improve your golf game through practice. It is this *approach* that will deliver you from novice to fifteen handicapper, from fifteen to five, and from five to scratch.

Along the way, you'll learn the many unwritten rules, mannerisms, and shibboleths of real golfers. *Let the Big Dog Eat* includes snippets of golf ephemera to steep you in the rich cultural history. I intentionally wrote this book in the vernacular of regular golfers.[4] My hope is that by knowing all this, new and longtime golfers will feel comfortable walking onto any course and finding their place there.

---

4 And maybe that language is coarse at times. This book has curses and insults, because that's the world of golf I know. Where I come from, cursing is part of the game, and it is all intended to be in good fun here.

GOLF BOOKS

When I was very young, first teaching myself to be a decent golfer, I read all the books written by golf legends. Harvey Penick's *Little Red Book*, Tiger Woods's *How I Play Golf*, Jack Nicklaus's *Golf My Way*, and, most famous of all, Ben Hogan's *Five Lessons*. I took in these tomes reverentially, trying to adopt all their techniques. After many years, though, I realized that that was impossible. All these icons swing differently, grip the club differently, approach the game differently, and absorbing their knowledge on its own got me no closer to beating my dad or winning high school matches.

Take Hogan—the greatest ball-striker who ever lived. Emulating his swing will fuck you up. That dude was five foot six and had a compact move. He would tell people that the "secret" of his swing was cupping his wrist, as if by copying that anyone could do what he did. How many golfers tried this and failed, I dare not say. I'll tell you the real secret: being Ben Hogan. You can't do what he did, and neither can anyone else.

This isn't to say that I didn't learn anything from those books. Obviously, I did.[5] I've developed my understanding of the game in part by absorbing all they had to teach. But you aren't Tiger Woods, Jack Nicklaus, or Ben Hogan. Their approach probably can't be your approach.[6]

---

5 And you should read them next after you finish this one.
6 Understand that if you're going to be the best player in the world, you probably have a pretty good idea that you might be by the time you're twelve. When I was in high school, I sometimes played tournaments against another kid from my

My book is for you.

Over the years, I've come to one core understanding of the game: you have to teach yourself. When you get a lesson, read a book, or watch a video, you can take away the knowledge to build your game, but you play the game alone.

To that end, this book is an omnibus account of all aspects of the game. You can use it start to finish to guide your progression. Take its lessons and add your own foibles, ideas, drills, and techniques. Adopt my philosophy if it appeals to you. If it doesn't, develop your own.

Why should you listen to me? Well, I am, wherever I have a few months to practice, an about-scratch golfer. I've traveled the world, played great courses, and played well there. Playing one group behind former president George W. Bush at Cape Arundel Golf Course in Maine, I shot 73. To me, this means I beat him. You should listen to me because I beat the President of the United States.

I didn't get here idly, either. When I started this journey, I basically sucked. I told you about being sixteen and beating balls on the driving range until my hands bled. It wasn't all roses. I would stand up there and slice drive after drive, and all the while this old head

---

town. We were similarly skilled players at the time, and I beat him once. Only one problem: I was seventeen and he was twelve. He went on to win the New England Amateur and play far more competitive golf than me. Understand, though, that despite being far more talented than me, he isn't playing on the PGA Tour today. If you're as talented as me, I probably can't teach you to be better than that kid, any more than I can teach him to be better than Jordan Spieth. I can teach you, any of you, to be a lot better than you are now, and that's as much as anyone will ever be able to give you.

named Tubby would sit behind me and yell over and over, "Keep your head down."[7]

Learning to play was, at times, humiliating. I couldn't hit the ball straight, I duffed every chip, and I missed all my short putts. I was often ashamed to play at all. Eventually, though, using the techniques in this book, I became a skilled player. That journey is what qualifies me to teach you.

I may not be Harvey Penick, but I've given my share of lessons. Sometimes, I took a strong golfer and helped them improve. Sometimes I took a complete neophyte and molded them in my own image.

One of my closest friends, Chet Lester, was my caddy when he started playing. Chet suckled at the teat of my golfing wisdom for years and grew from a helpless amoeba to a good golfer. Young Chet even beat me once last year, despite coming to the game much later in life than I did. This success was thanks to his own deliberate practice, of course, but my lessons worked their magic.

I've spent a lifetime watching bad golfers up close, and so I've seen the remarkably consistent mistakes they make. These are probably the mistakes you make. I'll explain how to identify and deal with them throughout this book.

---

7 Class isn't in session yet, but I would be remiss if I didn't take this opportunity to note that the age-old advice "keep your head down" is the most useless piece of shit advice anyone can give in the game of golf. If anyone tells you that you just need to keep your head down, they have no idea what the fuck they're talking about, and you can safely disregard them. I'll return to this in my chapter on the swing.

This book is not just about swinging, chipping, and putting; it's about playing golf. Maybe you understand the difference now, but you will for sure after you read this book. Like in life, the most successful golfers always keep learning and improving, and you should do the same.

The game of golf isn't just the sum of your shots. It's about you, out on the course alone. There are moments in this game when golfers can achieve perfect flow. In communion with the course. Those of us who have played long enough all know this feeling. From Purpoodock to Pinehurst to Penmar, I suggest that you cherish every shot you take. One of them, someday, will be your last.

CONTENTS

This book starts with a brief history of the game of golf and some of its champions, and then it follows an instructional arc designed to help any golfer improve. First, it teaches you how I think about the golf swing, its constituent parts, and how to learn it and improve. Next, it teaches you how to chip. Then, how to putt. After that, I expound on the skill of "scoring." These are strategies that will improve your carded numbers.

Once those core skills are established, I provide some thoughts on how to practice and techniques that players of any skill level can use to improve. These skills are useful to me every day, and I hope they can be for you too.

I close the book with a discussion of odds and ends like getting fitted for equipment and games like skins and Nassau. For new golfers, I include a robust discussion of formal and informal golf etiquette. Remember, though, I'm not coming from some fancy country club tradition. These are the rules of golf as I understand them, and they might not pertain everywhere you go.

I've chosen not to include any drawings in this book. This is primarily because I don't think drawings are a good way to understand what happens in a golf swing. I would love to present my book as a one-stop shop for everything you need to learn golf, but the truth is that no book could ever be that. This is a *conceptual* framework so that you know what's happening in the golf swing, but it must be paired with actual practice to be useful. My advice to you, if you read something I said and want to understand it, is to (1) put your hands on a club and give it a try, and (2) find videos of someone swinging as your guide. YouTube is a more complete compendium of the golf swing than anything I could hope to include in these pages. You should use it.

I hope that after reading this book, new golfers will find the onion layers of golf peeled back, the game's complexity demystified. This background should salve the twinge of anxiety that I see many new players feel on the golf course. For those golfers who have been out here for a while and already know a thing or two, this book will still help you improve. Let's go get it.

CHAPTER 1

THE HISTORY OF GOLF

BEFORE LEARNING GOLF, YOU SHOULD KNOW THAT IT'S AN ANCIENT game. Step onto any really old course, and you can almost feel the history burbling up out of the turf. For some people, this is a turnoff; the norms of the game seem antiquated and hostile. Part of the purpose of this book is to unlock the customs and shibboleths that can make golf seem impenetrable. Knowing a little history is part of that.

In my view, golf history is something worth celebrating. *Let the Big Dog Eat* isn't a history book, but a little background will help you contextualize its lessons. More than that, knowing some of this history is itself a discursive threshold for new golfers. Understanding just this basic background will set you on an even footing to participate fully in the game when you are out on the course.

It's sometimes said that the earliest recorded mention of the game is in the Scottish Act of Parliament of 1457, which banned playing "ye golf," purportedly because it was seen as a distraction from archery practice. It's clear, however, that some form of the game preceded this mention.

I once heard someone say that golf was invented because men were too afraid to ask each other to go for a walk. Thus far, my research has been unable to confirm or deny the truth of this story.

ANCIENT TIMES

There are drawings and paintings depicting golf-like games played in various parts of the world in ancient times. For example, drawings of a game called chuiwan show people playing a ball-and-stick game in ancient China. Chuiwan may have originated as early as the Han dynasty (206 BCE–220 CE).[8] The Romans may have also played a game called paganica, which resembled golf in some ways, involving hitting a feather-filled ball with a bent stick.[9] In either case, real old![10]

---

[8] If you're ever in Philadelphia or in New York's East Village, the restaurant Han Dynasty comes highly recommended. When we were young, we called it "Handy Nasty," and I hope you will too.

[9] Though every source for this game refers to the *Encyclopaedia Britannica*, casting some doubt as to its truth.

[10] Britannica, s.v. "golf," accessed April 3, 2024, https://www.britannica.com/sports/golf.

LET THE BIG DOG EAT

The origin of the word *golf* itself is hotly disputed by etymology buffs. One theory involves the Dutch word *kolf*, which means "club" and denoted a popular game in the Netherlands going back hundreds of years. According to this theory, the game of golf was introduced to Scotland by Dutch traders in the fifteenth century, and the name is derived from *kolf*, handed over by some frisky rogue. Another theory looks to the Scottish words *Goff*, *gowf*, *golf*, *goif*, *goiff*, *gof*, *gowfe*, *gouff*, and *glove*,[11] which mean "to strike or cuff." According to this theory, the bastardized *golf* refers to hitting the ball with a club. Similar games were also apparently played elsewhere in Europe around the same time.

ST ANDREWS

In any event, the modern game is thought to have been developed in Scotland. The town of St Andrews and the Old Course there are generally considered the birthplace of the modern game and often visited by players from around the world as a sort of fun boozy pilgrimage. The Old Course is thought to have been in existence since the fifteenth century, and in 1522 it was granted a charter by one Archbishop John Hamilton to officially permit "playing at golf,

---

11 Scottish Golf History, "Golf, Meaning of the Word Golf," accessed April 3, 2024, https://www.scottishgolfhistory.org/origin-of-golf-terms/golf.

futball, schuting at all gamis, with all uther maner of pastyme as ever thai plais."[12]

St Andrews is home to the Royal and Ancient Golf Club of St Andrews, one of the world's oldest and most influential golf clubs. The R&A was founded in 1754 and is responsible for establishing and enforcing the rules of golf worldwide.[13] These R&A rules are observed in much competition outside the United States (where USGA Rules of Golf, discussed in a later chapter, are followed).

OLD TOM MORRIS

Professional golf as a sport has been played since the late nineteenth century. The first professional golf tournament was the Open Championship (sometimes called the British Open), which was first played in 1860 and won by one Willie Park Sr.[14]

Park's competitor, and the first true professional golfer, was "Old" Tom Morris. Morris was born in St Andrews in 1821, and he learned to play golf as a young boy on the St Andrews Links. From 1861 to 1867, he won the Open Championship four times.

---

12 Golf Monthly, "Is St. Andrews the World's Oldest Golf Course?" May 6, 2022, https://www.golfmonthly.com/features/is-st-andrews-the-worlds-oldest-golf-course.

13 The Royal and Ancient Golf Club of St Andrews, accessed April 3, 2024, https://www.randa.org/en/the-royal-and-ancient-golf-club.

14 The Open, "1860/Prestwick," accessed April 3, 2024, https://www.theopen.com/previous-opens/1st-open-prestwick-1860#overview.

In addition to his success as a golfer, Morris literally made the clubs that elites at the time played with.[15] Not one to leave well enough alone, he also designed many of the courses still played today, including the 1st and 18th holes at the Old Course.[16] At the same time, Morris helped popularize golf in America and the world, mentoring many architects who would be influential beyond Scotland, including A. W. Tillinghast and C. B. Macdonald.[17]

His son Young Tom Morris was the next important golfer. Young Tom was born in 1851 and, given his obvious familial intimacy with the game, began playing at a young age. He won the Open Championship four times in a row, from 1868 to 1872 (there was no championship in 1871), and still holds the record for the lowest score in the tournament, 174 in 1869. Tragically, after losing his wife and newborn, he died of a broken heart (no shit) at age twenty-four in 1875.[18]

GOLF IN THE UNITED STATES

Around the same time Young Tom Morris died, golf came to the United States. The US has been responsible for much of the game's

---

15 National Records of Scotland, "Old Tom Morris and Young Tom Morris," accessed April 3, 2024, https://www.nrscotland.gov.uk/research/learning/features/old-tom-morris-and-young-tom-morris.

16 National Records of Scotland.

17 *Links Magazine*, "The Brilliance of Old Tom Morris," accessed May 20, 2024, https://linksmagazine.com/the-brilliance-of-old-tom-morris.

18 National Records of Scotland.

flourishing since the nineteenth century, and a strong plurality of the world's best players in that time have been born here. In one telling, the first golf course established in the United States was the Oakhurst Links in White Sulfur Springs, West Virginia, founded in 1884.[19] In another, the first golf in the United States took place in 1888 in Yonkers, New York, at a course established by the Scotsman John Reid.[20]

In any case, the first professional tournament in the US was the US Open, held in Newport, Rhode Island, in 1895.[21] The United States Golf Association was founded in 1894 to act as a governing body for the game.[22] To this day, the USGA rules are the American counterpoint to the R&A rules followed elsewhere.

Donald Ross was the first essential figure in American golf. An apprentice of Old Tom Morris himself and a greenskeeper at the Old Course from a young age, the Scottish-born Ross moved to the United States in 1899.[23] Immediately, his work as golf course designer and

---

19 See Oakhurt Links National Registry of Historic Places Registration Form, October 11, 2001, https://wvculture.org/wp-content/uploads/2021/03/Oakhurst -links.pdf.

20 *The Scotsman*, "The History of How Scotland Brought Golf to America," accessed April 3, 2024, https://www.scotsman.com/news/the-history-of-how -scotland-brought-golf-to-america-1481136.

21 United States Golf Association, "U.S. Open Results: 1895 to Present," accessed April 3, 2024, https://www.usga.org/content/usga/home-page/media/online -media-center/usga-records/u-s--open-results--1895-to-present.html.

22 United States Golf Association, "Celebrating 120 Years of the USGA: Part 1—A Nation Is Introduced to Golf," December 2014, https://www.usga.org /content/usga/home-page/articles/2014/12/celebrating-120-years-of-the-usga -part-1-a-nation-is-introduced-to-golf-21474873960.html.

23 Links, "The Accessible Donald Ross," June 18, 2014, https://linksmagazine .com/the_accessible_donald_ross.

builder influenced the game here. Ross designed hundreds of American courses, and even today his designs carry a certain gravitas.

Some of the best-known courses designed by Ross include Pinehurst No. 2 in North Carolina, Oak Hill Country Club in New York, and Portland Country Club in Maine. These courses are considered among the best in the country and have hosted numerous US Opens. Odds are good that if you play golf long enough east of the Mississippi, you will encounter more than a few Donald Ross courses. Know his name.

PROFESSIONAL GOLF

While Donald Ross was building, professional golfers in the United States were popularizing the sport among the masses. None was as influential early in golf's evolution as Bobby Jones. Jones was born in 1902 in Atlanta, Georgia, and was an immediate star. Jones won thirteen major championships during his career, including four US Opens, three Open Championships, and five US Amateur titles. He is one of only five players to have won all four majors, which is known as a "Grand Slam," though this was made up of different tournaments in those days. His celebrity fueled the growth of the game in the twentieth century, getting a ticker tape parade in Manhattan for his accomplishments. Later in life, he cofounded the Masters Tournament, which is now one of the four majors, the most prestigious golf tournaments in the world.[24] He even helped develop Augusta National Golf Club, which hosts the Masters. Ever since, that tournament has been synonymous with his legacy.

His career was relatively short, and after Jones retired from competitive golf in 1930, a number of new golfers sprang up to expand the game even more. These include Ben Hogan, who dominated the 1940s and 1950s; Arnold Palmer, whose charisma and charm won over America in the 1950s and 1960s; and Jack Nicklaus, who achieved new levels of dominance by winning major championships in the 1960s, 1970s, and 1980s.

Ben Hogan was born in 1912 in Stephenville, Texas—one of the first Texans in a long tradition of great golfers from the Lone Star State. He was famous for his dedication, discipline, and rough demeanor. When I was a kid, I read about the endless hours he spent perfecting his technique. Even though Hogan is long since dead, I nonetheless heard stories about him wherever I went. He was known for his attention to detail and constant refinement of his swing. Even as a small man, he was the longest hitter of his day, and one of the most accurate ever. He was famous for flagging shots in major tour-

---

24 The four current majors are the Open Championship, the US Open, the Masters Tournament, and the PGA Championship. Historically, the US Amateur and British Amateur were considered majors, but this designation faded at some point in the late twentieth century. Still, if you watch old broadcasts, you will sometimes hear announcers stating idiosyncratic major counts. When Bobby Jones was winning majors, the amateur championships were definitively considered majors. However, at a certain point, professional golf eclipsed the amateur game, and the two ams were downgraded slightly. Nonetheless, winners and contenders at the amateur championships frequently go on to be successful pros, and winning multiple times is a good indicator of future greatness (see Jack Nicklaus and Tiger Woods).

naments to put daggers in the hearts of his opponents. Today, he's generally considered the greatest ball-striker who ever lived.[25]

While never known as a great putter, Hogan was so dominant striking the ball that he was able to win nine major championships during his career, including five US Opens, two Masters, and one Open Championship. Six of these came after his entire lower body was shattered by a Greyhound bus in 1949. Hogan was the most acclaimed player of his time, and his book *Five Lessons,* published in 1957, is the most important book on golf ever written.

After age and injuries hobbled Hogan, the next great American golfer was Arnold Palmer. Palmer was known for his aggressive play and blue-collar popularity with fans. In sharp contrast to Hogan's tight, controlled swing, Palmer's was wild. Coming out of the hills of western Pennsylvania (and the Coast Guard), he thrashed at the ball and paced the course with swashbuckling swagger. Fans loved him for it, and until Tiger, he might have been the preeminent icon of the sport. Palmer won seven majors during his career, including four Masters and two Open Championships. He never won the PGA championship, which, to be fair, was not as prestigious at the time. To compensate, the beverage made by mixing one part iced tea and one part lemonade has been named after him.[26]

Palmer carried the torch of golf in the United States until Jack Nicklaus emerged as the new alpha in the 1960s. Nicklaus won a record eighteen major championships during his career, along with

---

25 Fun fact, my dad wanted to name me Ben Hogan Brogan. Missed opportunity.

26 The story goes that Palmer added a third part of vodka to his personal mix.

73 PGA Tour wins (and several US Amateurs). Nicklaus, from Ohio, was less svelte and composed than many of his contemporaries. This led Palmer to be, at first, taken aback at losing to the kid he called "Fat Jack." Ultimately, Jack's raw physical talent, tireless work ethic, and dogged competitive fire made him probably the greatest golfer ever. He won his majors over a twenty-three-year span, and people forget that he was in real competition to win the 1998 Masters at the age of fifty-eight, finishing tied for sixth.[27] In addition to winning the most majors, he also came in *second* the most times. Nicklaus has also become a leading designer of golf courses after his retirement from the game and is known for his difficult, persnickety, layouts.

After Jack won the 1986 Masters, golf entered a doldrum for some time. The legends of the game faded into the background, and also-rans like Greg Norman were unable to take up their mantle. This changed when a skinny kid named Eldrick began winning US Amateur tournaments in the early 1990s. Eldrick Tont "Tiger" Woods was born in Cypress, California, on December 30, 1975. He began playing golf at a young age and quickly developed into a skilled player. By 1978, at the age of three, he was on TV putting against Bob Hope, and his military father pushed him mercilessly in the hope of making him the greatest golfer of all time. It worked.[28] Tiger won three US Amateurs in a row and then turned professional

---

27 Among the most impressive age-related accomplishments in golf, perhaps trailing only Tom Watson's second-place finish at the Open Championship in 2009 at age fifty-nine and Phil Mickelson's stunning win at the PGA Championship at Kiawah at age fifty-one in 2021.

28 Sort of.

LET THE BIG DOG EAT

in 1996 to immediately make a name for himself on the professional golf circuit.

Nobody plays golf like Tiger. He hit the ball farther than anyone, could pull off any shot, chipped the ball better than anyone, never missed a short putt, and was the best in the world at draining the long ones when it counted. Nobody anywhere disputes that when Tiger was at his peak, he was the best golfer who ever lived.

In 1997, Woods won his first major championship, the Masters, while lapping the field by an unheard-of twelve strokes. He went on to win fifteen major championships, the second-most ever, and was once on pace to win far more than Jack.

For everything, though, there is a price, and years of military discipline and celebrity took their toll on Tiger. On Thanksgiving 2009, Tiger drove his SUV into a mailbox as his wife, Elin, chased him, and soon after, his body and mind broke down. He made a number of comebacks and was even the best player in the world again at times, but his ascendency ended that night.

Some of his most notable wins include lapping the field at Pebble Beach in the 2000 US Open to win by fifteen strokes; the Tiger Slam, when he held all four major titles concurrently for a period in 2002; his playoff victory over Rocco Mediate on a bum leg at the 2008 US Open at Torrey Pines; and his comeback win at the 2019 Masters.

Tiger's ascendency ushered in a new era of the game. His influence on the modern game has been profound, and he individually raised the profile of the game and brought in legions of new fans. Before Tiger, golf was seen as a stodgy old country club sport played by out-of-shape white boys. Tiger oozed energy and vitality and created a space for the young cocky athletes who have moved the game forward ever since.

After Tiger's career was derailed by injuries, drugs, and serial infidelity in the early 2010s, a new generation of talent arose in his place. The charisma of players like Jordan Spieth and Rory McIlroy has made the game (very nearly) as popular as ever, even without a dominant force to fill Tiger's shoes.

In 2020, when the COVID-19 pandemic came and ruined our lives for a little while, golf exploded in popularity. For many people, it was the only recreation they could do. Out in the fields, in God's fresh air, we walked together as the world burned. Now here we are putting together the pieces, and golf is still here. Currently professional golf is in a struggle between the PGA Tour and the LIV Tour. What comes next is anyone's guess.

Note that this brief lesson has ignored many golf legends like Gene Sarazen, Tom Watson, and John Daly, as well as architects, courses, and traditions worldwide. I've also glossed over the entire professional women's game, which has its own storied history. Once you start playing, you'll absorb more of these legends, apocryphal and real. This chapter is only meant to give you a little bit of background before we dive in. Now to play.

CHAPTER 2

SETTING UP

GOLF IS A GAME OF SWINGS, AND THE FULL GOLF SWING IS THE THING we all love most. A beautiful golf swing makes our romantic partners swoon as our competitors look on in awe. Watch a young Ernie Els swing, and you feel something. The power and grace of the big man moving the club so smoothly while transferring so much energy into that little white ball. Other sexy swingers you might have heard of include Freddie Couples, Michelle Wie, and Tommy Fleetwood. Joe LaCava, Freddie's former caddy, spent decades prescreening women who had seen Couples's smooth move and wanted a piece of the action. You want your bosses, friends, and cart girls[29] to feel the same way about you.

---

29 This is a joke. Cart girls don't like you at all. Please don't harass them, it's creepy. Tip well and shut the fuck up.

Spend enough time around golf, and you'll probably hear the phrase "drive for show, putt for dough." It's meant to convey the idea that while hitting the ball hard and pure may well be the charismatic part of the game, it's the yeoman's work on and around the greens that really counts. As I discuss in the chapter that deals with scoring, putting is really important. That said, I think the old putt-for-dough adage is overstated. Putting moderately well is pretty easy, fundamentally. You could take any idiot with no experience and teach them to reliably two-putt after a few weeks of practice on the green. Not so with hitting the ball.

The golf swing is a complex, difficult, and ungainly movement that takes a long period of dedicated practice to do with any degree of competency. Your task in golf is to start some 400 yards away from a tiny hole, stand over a tiny ball, and hit your ball into that hole in as few shots as possible. You have a lot of ground to cover, so if you want to play golf well, you have to start with strong ball-striking.

On a certain level, golf swings are ineffable. The swing is so fast and complicated that I don't think anyone can fully conceptualize the biomechanics at play in the complete action. If you think about it, most physical action exists in the subconscious. How do you run? If you're like me, you just put on your shoes and do it. You can practice your form at the margins, but, at ground, the motion is intuitive. The golf swing is the same way, except most people find it *unintuitive.*

A corollary to this, I believe, is that the golf swing can't be learned just by describing how it happens. This conceit is core to learning

LET THE BIG DOG EAT

golf well. Reading about the sequence of motions in the swing, on its own, won't meaningfully advance you toward playing good golf. Because the golf swing exists largely in the subconscious, I can't tell you how to "do" a golf swing in any way that would be immediately actionable for you. Golf swings can only be built over time through careful repetition and effort. Trial and error. Observation and practice.

The golf swing is "emergent," meaning that it can't be described in terms of its components alone. The swing only becomes a swing when performed in fluid rhythm. If you break it down into component parts, it becomes impossible to perform. From an instructional standpoint, this means that lessons are generally a degree of abstraction removed. We will work in concepts, but these are just cues. When it comes to the swing, you just do it. The whole is out of your control, so you have to slowly accrete skill to your form. Like I said, the swing is a little ineffable, which means I can't quite tell you how to do it, but I can sure as hell teach you how to learn it through deliberate practice.

The following chapters teach you how to swing the golf club well. First, I provide an in-depth description of good setup. When you have so little deliberate control over each swing, the one thing you can control, setup, takes outsize importance. After that, I walk you through the swing, from backswing to follow-through, and add notes on spin, trajectory, and other more advanced concepts.

By understanding how each element of the swing is supposed to work, you will have a foundation to begin to mold your own swing to the ideal. Don't expect this to happen in one range session. A golf swing takes time to build. If you take these concepts to heart, though, and train them deliberately, over time you will find yourself hitting the ball better and better, and will be well on the way to playing good golf.

SETUP

The most fundamental aspect of the golf swing comes before the club starts to move. Whenever I teach a new golfer how to play, I start with setup. When I am trying to help golfers out on the course, I usually start here. This is not because there's one correct setup that must be followed to play good golf. On the contrary, I think this area of the game is highly variable, and good golf can be played from any number of postures.

However, a good, fundamentally sound setup forms an excellent basis for a good, fundamentally sound golf swing. Setup is the *one* aspect of the golf swing that the golfer can control completely with the conscious mind. This makes setup an incredibly powerful tool because it allows the easiest on-course self-evaluation and correction, which can save a failing round.

Beyond being easy to correct midround, for good players, setup can be a tool to compensate for more complicated issues. Lee Trevino blocked the shit out of the golf ball, hitting balls that started right and stayed right. If he lined up straight on his target line, he would miss right every time, so he didn't do that. He aimed left of the target, and he won six majors doing it. I almost never see players do this on the golf course, but many of us absolutely should. You can't manipulate your setup to hack your swing like Lee Trevino if you don't know what your baseline is, so learning to set up consistently is a fundamental skill that all good golfers should master.

Because setup is the one thing you can always control, you should build the habit of always practicing and playing with the same setup. As an ancillary benefit, this can make you a more clutch player. Routine helps you maintain consistency under pressure. The ritual of going through your setup can help you settle into a routine and alleviate nerves out on the golf course. Just like Steph Curry going through his free throw routine, consistent setup will ease you into your swing.

All this is to say, you should think about your setup every time you hit a golf ball, in practice, on the course, in competition. Every single time. If you don't already think about your setup, good news! Just by doing that, you will become a materially better golfer. So where should setup begin?

CHOOSE YOUR SHOT

Before anything else, when you begin your setup, you must evaluate your position, be it on the tee, in the fairway, in the rough, or under the trees, and choose a shot you want to hit. I discuss this further in the strategy section of chapter 7, but you should know now that your setup cannot begin until you've chosen a shot. Everything you do will be dictated by the shot you choose. Ball placement, stance, and grip will change depending on whether you want to hit a high cut or a low hook. To hit golf shots well, you have to play with conviction, and to play with conviction, you must choose a shot.

Once you've chosen your shot, pick a target—a specific spot to aim for. I like to choose the top of a tree or something similarly distinct. If asked, you should be able to articulate exactly what you're aiming for. Next, with that aim point in mind, look at your target and visualize your shot approaching.

Having done all that and knowing what you will do, you can now begin the physical portion of the setup.

BALL PLACEMENT

The start of your setup has nothing to do with your body at all. At the start of each hole, on the tee box, you will have the option of placing your ball on a tee. The position of the ball on the tee is the first thing you can control, and you should leverage it to your advantage.

When asked why he teed up the ball for wedge and short iron shots from the tee box, Jack Nicklaus famously said, "Because I play golf for a living." While I see Jack's point, I disagree that this must apply in every situation. I tend to hit the ball very high with the short clubs and can get lower spinny shots more easily from the turf, so I think there are some situations where tees don't make sense. Then again, Jack won eighteen majors and I am an attorney, so I will let you decide whom to believe.

LET THE BIG DOG EAT

I can't tell you what the right way to set up the ball on the tee is for you. Broadly, though, the most common approach is to tee the ball up half of a ball above the top of the club when hitting driver, and down close to the turf with irons and other woods. When I hit long irons, I like to tee the ball up a smidge higher to ensure a higher ball flight and softer landing, even if my strike isn't perfect, but your preferences may differ. Try different approaches, and then adopt a consistent routine at the tee, placing your ball down in the best way that suits the shot you intend to hit.

The routine itself is important and something I'll continue to stress in this book. In golf, your nerves, and thus your conscious mind where they lurk, are your enemy. Adopting a consistent routine will help you keep your approach subconscious where it belongs and help you perform at your best.

While teeing up your ball may seem so simple as to be trivial, I see mediocre golfers fuck up over and over again. According to the rules of golf, you have the entire width between the tee markers and two club lengths back from that line to place your ball.[30] That's a big space and you can tee up your ball anywhere inside it. Use it! Poor golfers seem to always place their balls on uneven, rough, wet, or disadvantageous turf. Don't do this! Instead, think your way around the tee box. If you can avoid it, don't place your ball behind a tree or low-hanging branch either. Clear shots from good turf are easier to execute, and this is your one chance to guarantee that.

---

30 I have a friend who always tees the ball up in front of the tees—don't do this. It's cheating, even if only in a minor way.

In addition to making this game harder for yourself, there's a little extra incentive here as well. If you do mess this up, you risk revealing to all the real golfers in your group that you're a moron. This is your one chance per hole to place the ball somewhere good. Take advantage. Tee the ball in good grass unobstructed and visualize the shot you will hit from there.

One note: some players seem to think they can improve their lies *away from the tee box* as well. You should know that the rules do not permit you to select your ball placement elsewhere. Play the ball as it lies. Anything else is cheating.[31]

If you're so inclined to move your ball around, you may think you're getting away with it, but you aren't. Everyone who plays golf knows who the cheaters are. If you're one of them, no one will ever trust you in any avenue of life. Cheat on your wife, cheat on your taxes, cheat at golf. Don't be that person. We will all make fun of you behind your back.

With that aside, you're ready to step up to the ball.

---

31 Unless moving the ball is permitted by the rules; for example, if you lie in casual water or on a day the golf course is playing lift, clean, replace. If allowed by the rules, you can and should move your ball, and the same advice as on the tee box applies. Find good ground, don't put yourself behind a tree. It's a good idea if you're taking a legal drop or placing your ball that you inform your opponent first of your situation and ask for a ruling on whether you can drop/place the ball. Always be generous in granting this in casual competition. In serious competition, you're entitled to consult the rules or an official and play accordingly, but never create a hassle for your opponent if the rule is clear. In casual competition, if your opponent is being stingy with drops, spit in their drink and make them putt out all their 2-footers. They just don't get it.

ADDRESS

You've assessed your lie and chosen your shot, so now it's time to step up to the ball. As I mentioned earlier, there's no single way to do this. There are, however, some general principles for addressing the ball that I teach because I think they're good jumping-off points.

Position the ball around the middle of your feet for your stock full-swing iron shot. Your legs should be roughly shoulder width, weighted 60/40 toward your lead leg (this is the left leg for right-handed golfers, and the right leg for left-handed golfers). You don't want to be up on the balls of your feet, but you don't want to be on your heels either. Balanced is good. Knees should be slightly bent, and your torso should be hinged slightly forward from your hips. A good physical cue for this position (if you've played other sports) is the defensive stance in basketball or a fielding position in baseball. Your stance at address should be similar to that, though perhaps a touch more upright.

Note that there's substantial room for variation in your posture at address. Bryson DeChambeau steps up to the ball like it stole his girl, and he won the US Open, so my way isn't the only way.[32] Your best bet is to develop your own approach to this posture, but you should be conscious of what you're doing.[33] An athletic posture will serve you well.

---

32 It's just the best way.

33 Tiger likes to keep his glutes active. I don't know what that means. Proceed with caution.

Once you have your feet set comfortably, you can start to think about upper body position. First, though, I think getting a club in your hands and thinking about your grip is a good idea.

To grip the club, place it in your (gloved) nondominant hand, balancing the weight between the first segment of your index finger and the fat part of the palm of your hand. The club should feel stable in this position. If the club feels unstable in your gloved hand, you should make slight adjustments until it's steady. Some people may not have strong-enough wrists and hands to hold it stable in this position. Unfortunately, if that's the case, you're in for bigger issues down the road, but do your best here.

Once you have the club in this position, wrap the fingers of your nondominant hand around it naturally. Make sure that the clubhead is facing close to straight ahead (such that it is parallel to your body when you stand straight up and hold the shaft at a 90-degree angle from your hips), with the clubface perpendicular to your intended target line. Now, add your dominant hand to the club and align your thumbs so that both are pointing down the club's shaft, with the pinkie of your dominant hand either overlapping or interlocking with the index finger of your nondominant hand. Congrats! You have gripped the club!

Historically, most golfers have overlapped, but Jack interlocked, and Tiger copied him, so now most young golfers interlock. In my opinion, it doesn't matter very much which style you choose. I like to interlock because it feels secure to me, but Jim Furyk uses a goddamn claw grip. If you already have a weird grip and it's working for you, that might be okay, but you definitely want a secure purchase on the club. Your hands should be together so that they can rotate through the shot readily, and the clubface with your hands out naturally in front of you should be close to perpendicular to your target line.[34]

Now, with the club in hand, let your arms hang down naturally, which should place the clubhead evenly on the ground.[35] You can move your feet slightly forward or back to get the clubhead directly behind the ball. This position is known as "address."

The distance you stand from the ball is critical to your ability to make solid contact. But there's no way for me to tell you where exactly the right place for you to stand is. You will have to figure out what works best for you and then endeavor to be completely consistent.

I will repeat this throughout this book, but consistency is essential to effective practice. Consistency, by giving you a predictable starting point, allows you to adjust components of your swing as needed when your swing starts to go wrong. Be consistent in your ball position, and you will find it easier to improve other, more complex parts of your game. For a more complete guide to evaluating your position relative to the ball, reference chapter 8 on how

---

34 Most golfers do not hold the club perfectly perpendicular to the target line. If the face is slightly closed to the line, that's called a strong grip. And if it's open, that's a weak grip. Opinions differ on which one is better, and this is one of the first things that I will manipulate when something is going wrong with my swing. This is why it's so important to have a well-understood, consistent setup, because that baseline allows you to consciously manipulate elements of your setup to correct issues midround or in your practice sessions.

35 Assuming that your clubs are well fit to you, see chapter 4 on equipment for more on this topic.

to practice. Note also that the distance you stand from the ball will differ for each club, since the clubs are different lengths.

If you've listened to my advice to this point, you should be in an athletic stance, club gripped firmly in your hands and positioned behind the ball. Next, check that the rest of your upper body is well positioned to make an athletic move. Generally, you want your head to be over the ball, although depending on the position of the ball in your stance, your head may be slightly behind it. In my opinion, it's more important that your overall balance be stable than your head be directly over the ball. This position of your head and the effect it has on your overall balance is another aspect of your swing that you may want to play with a little bit until you find a place where you're comfortable and consistent.

Even if you can't perfect all these elements of the setup right away, it's important to know and remember that all these variables exist. That way, during your practice sessions and play, you will have a conceptual framework to incorporate your thoughts and observations. Your setup and approach must be personal to you. If you don't know the elements of your own setup, you will be unable to fix them when the time comes.

If these details seem overwhelming or excessive, the key is to remember that you won't have to think about them all the time. Drill good and consistent habits into your swing during practice. Then, you'll be prepared when the pressure rises during competition, and stress inhibits your focus and control. Turn good setup into a habit, rehearse it completely before you enter competition, and you'll be able to maintain your fundamentals and play well under pressure.

MEASURE YOURSELF

For consistency in setup, "feel" is often not enough. I recommend practicing with empirical tools to further drill these habits in correctly during practice. Your understanding of your setup is fallible, but a stick on the ground never will be.

When you "feel" your swing, you use a sense called "proprioception," which is a little wonky. Your proprioceptive feeling is good at telling you if your body is varying from the patterns you're used to, but it's not good at giving you an absolute sense of what your body is actually doing in space.

Take, for example, Jim Furyk. If you know golf, you know that he's known for his batshit looping swing, which he and his dad developed organically in the hills of western Pennsylvania. As weird as his swing is, Furyk has said in interviews that until he made the tour and saw himself on TV, he never knew how atypical it was. This wasn't because Jim Furyk didn't understand golf or know what a good swing looked like; he couldn't "feel" that his swing was nontraditional because proprioception didn't evolve to calibrate golf swings. This same logic will apply to you. You cannot, fundamentally, feel what your body is actually doing in your golf swing. Because of this, if you rely on feel alone, you will find it difficult to improve. If you want to get better and become more consistent, you have to use external tools to measure and guide your swing during practice. Your brain will lie to you, a stick will not.

I believe that the best tools to guide your setup practice are surveying stakes, a video camera, and a tripod. You've probably noticed that the best players tend to have a stick or two down on the ground when they go to the range. The most important stick sits between you and the ball, and points in the direction where you want the ball to start its flight, that is, your target line. Some players, myself included, use a second stick to guide the position of the ball back to front in their stance. This stick should be set down perpendicular to your first stick, giving a visual guide for ball placement and setup.

Bougie golf courses will try to sell you branded sticks at absurd markups; don't fall into this trap. Go to your local hardware store and ask for two surveying sticks, six dollars, bada bing bada boom. You're in business. See chapter 8 on practice for more details, but internalize this: never practice full swings without at least one alignment stick down. Drill your alignment every time you practice so that you'll be dialed in every time you play. If you happen to not have your sticks during a practice session, you can place an iron on the ground instead, but be warned that your grip will probably get a little gross sitting there on the grass.

Beyond the sticks, the camera[36] and tripod, I hope, are self-explanatory. Take videos to see what the hell you're actually doing in

---

36 Feel free to use an iPhone camera. I do. Phones usually have a good slow-motion video feature, too, which is useful here.

the swing. The best angles for recording your golf swings are behind you down the line, facing you from the side, and facing your back. You can review these videos during the session to see if the changes you're trying to implement are working or in the film room (your car) later on to better understand your move. It's a pain to do this every time, especially early in your golf journey when you really just need reps more than anything else, but using the camera frequently will pay dividends. Remember, you can't feel what you are doing. If you want to build a fundamentally sound swing, you need empirical tools.

ON ALIGNMENT

Once you're comfortable with your setup, you should begin to think about the alignment of your body. There are two aspects to alignment: one is the alignment that different parts of your body have relative to each other. I prefer to have my feet, knees, hips, shoulders, and head aligned on a single plane, as though a pane of glass were running through my body. I stole that analogy from Ben Hogan (albeit repurposed). Shout-out to the GOAT.

The second aspect of alignment is your body's alignment with the target. Many different approaches to alignment may be successful for different players. While one approach is to point your body directly along the target line, I don't think that this is actually optimal all or even most of the time. As you learn how to hit specific shots for specific circumstances, you will realize that each one requires a slightly different alignment to the target.

In the realm of full swings, when you're hitting a draw or hook, a shot that (for a right-handed player) starts right of your target and, through spin, curves to the left in the air, you should *aim right* so that once the ball curves, it will end up on target. The opposite is true for a cut or slice, a shot that starts left (for a right-handed golfer) and then turns right in the air. Aim left so that the ball ends up on target.

Beyond these familiar old saws, you should remember that all of this is individualized too. When I hit a cut, I aim *way* left because I've noticed that when I swing for that specific shot, my ball tends to "push" or take a rightward trajectory off the clubface and spin to the right. If I don't compensate for this by aiming way off to the left, I'll never be on target when I hit these shots.

I think some fundamentals are actually fundamental, meaning that there is a right way to do them.[37] In the realm of alignment to the target,[38] however, I don't think it matters how you do it. There are a lot of approaches here that could conceivably be successful. Remember, Lee Trevino won six majors aiming far out to the left on every shot. A lot of amateurs would be uncomfortable taking such a dramatic approach, but some of them would be wrong to dismiss it. If your swing is repeatable, accurate, and getting you power, I don't give one shit where your aim is starting. Do whatever gets the ball on target. What really matters is consistency, so when you practice, learn the tendencies of your shots, and practice aiming accordingly.

---

37 Or at least a definitively wrong way.

38 This is opposed to alignment of the body to itself, which I think should almost always be straight as if through a pane of glass, as I described above.

LET THE BIG DOG EAT

FINAL NOTE ON SETUP

Drill this idea into your head: *there is no one right way.* Golf is a game of moving a small ball from a tee into a hole a great distance away while using as few swings as possible. Golf is not a game of achieving technical perfection or even aesthetic beauty. That stuff doesn't matter at all, friend. The sooner you can abandon the insipid ideal of technical perfection and build a setup that works for you, the sooner you soar.

While the specifics of your setup need not follow any specific path, what does really matter is that you (1) understand each aspect of a setup; (2) consider how manipulating those fundamentals affects your shots; and (3) practice your setup and manipulations to that setup until you develop muscle memory sufficient to execute consistently under pressure.

From there, you can continue to reassess and improve your swing or fix inconsistencies and problems that arise naturally. If you take nothing else from this book, remember that consistency is everything in golf. Doing the same thing every time keeps you out of trouble and gives you the confidence to take riskier shots. You must have a consistent setup to be a consistent golfer, so it all starts here. I have seen so many poor golfers dismiss this part of the game only to bemoan all their other issues with their swings. Fools. Start here, start stable, and build up. If you do all this, I guarantee that you will play better golf.

CHAPTER 3

THE SWING

NELLY KORDA STANDS BEFORE A BALL, WEIGHT EVENLY DISPERSED over both feet. She places the clubhead behind the ball. Nelly pulls the club back, up above and behind her head while rotating her torso. Without moving her feet,[39] she draws the club farther back. As her upper body twists and her arms pull the club back behind her head, Nelly's weight shifts slightly from neutral back onto her back foot. Her upper body moves slightly back in cadence with the weight transfer and rotation.

Reaching the top of the swing, the direction of the action changes. Nelly's feet begin to torque outward in the direction of the

---

39 Some foot movement is permissible. Jack Nicklaus, Bubba Watson, and Scottie Scheffler move their forward foot up off the ground to facilitate long, loopy backswings and generate more power. As a general rule, though, the more unstable your base, the more inconsistency you will introduce into your swing. If you are not Jack Nicklaus, Bubba Watson, or Scottie Scheffler, proceed with a live lead foot with caution.

golf shot, spikes digging into the turf, and the rotation is transferred and amplified through the knees and legs. The hips fire around and generate even more torque in the abdomen. This then transfers up farther through the shoulders and reverses the direction of the upper body rotation, which transfers into the club grip and shaft before violently redirecting the clubhead down at the ground.

The clubhead swings down, Nelly's arms extended, before making contact with the ball and exploding through it, imparting directional energy and spin on the ball, which is already away. Her arms clear in front of her body and swing up around, pulling the club up high around her head again. Her right foot comes up off the ground to accommodate the former center of mass rotation from the club, moving forward and away from the body. Finally, Nelly poses, standing upright, and with a serious expression watches her golf ball fly toward the target.

This is really fucking complicated, right? Compound that with the fact that all this takes place in around a second (unless you're Hideki Matsuyama, and even then, quickly), and you will understand why I say you absolutely cannot think your way through a golf swing. The superior cortex of my brain, which guides intentional actions, has no idea how to make a golf swing. No, these processes are guided by the deeply recessed lizard parts of your brain and informed by practice, not cognition.[40]

---

40 You may, if you're good, be able to have one, or at maximum two (to be honest, while some people say they have two swing thoughts, I think they're lying), swing thoughts, which guide some aspect of your move intentionally. Use this judiciously, though; most of your swing is below the surface of your mind.

We're lucky, though. Blessed because we intuitively understand this move. The motion of the golf swing comes to us as part of an uncanny genetic memory. Have you ever seen a cheetah run? Nobody taught cheetahs how to do that; they just know. Humans have the same talent for throwing, and a golf swing is a throw.

Now, of course, you're holding a club during the golf swing, and striking a stationary object on the ground, but the motion is the same. I like to think of the golf swing as throwing the clubhead at the ball. If you doubt me, practice throwing a baseball or skipping a stone a few times, then direct that motion toward a spot on the ground. You will find yourself in a rough simulacrum of the golf swing.

Adopt this perspective; I guarantee it will make it easier for you to feel your way through your swing naturally. You can use this "throwing" move to generate mostly predictable reactions from the ball and to play good golf. All you have to do is place the club in your hands and refine this intuitive movement, and soon you will see the ball zipping down the range.

MOVING THE CLUB

I want to stop briefly to repeat that the exact biomechanics of a golf swing will always be somewhat ineffable. A golf swing is too complicated and too fast to conceptualize fully. If you doubt me, watch your friend swing. Then, on his next shot, use the high-speed camera feature on your phone, record your friend's swing, and play it back.

In the slow-motion video that results, you will notice things about your friends' swings you have never seen in hours of watching them play live. The golf shaft bends behind them in their transition, their face contorts, and their feet and hips fire violently. In other words, when you watch a swing in the real world, you don't actually see it. Your brain processes the complex high-speed motion in front of you. It compresses it into a summary that your simple mind can understand.

As you make your move, numerous muscles fire in different directions, all minutely synchronized to generate a whip at the end of your hands, which in turn is transferred through the club and (hopefully) to the ball. Your brain has no way to internalize all these high-speed actions, so you experience them as a single swing. As you improve in golf, or at least as I've improved in golf, you develop a *feel* for your swing, and you can manipulate *that feel* to control your shots or even salvage a mistake. What you feel, though, isn't what you're actually doing. It's a compressed summary, just like what you see when you watch someone else's swing.

A golf swing is just fundamentally mysterious on some level, and don't let Bryson DeChambeau tell you any different. If you come to believe this, as I do, it will strengthen your game by helping you accept that, even in perfect conditions, randomness is baked into the game.

I have watched so many golfers ruin rounds trying to fix something they think is broken in their swing because of a bad shot or several bad shots they hit. I know, and you should too, that sometimes shots are bad for *no reason at all*. This is okay because your competitors face the same obstacle. Understanding this and accepting it will make you a mentally tougher golfer. Beating up on yourself over bad shots or missed putts will only hurt you in competition.

So what can we do to improve our game if the golf swing is mysterious and unfathomable? To become better ball-strikers, we must harness and refine our natural ability to throw the club through mindful practice, focusing on a few critical junctures in the swing.

To build a better swing, most golfers should focus on three things: (1) the takeaway, because this will define the position of the golf club at the top of the swing; (2) timing and the transition from backswing to the downswing, which, assuming your setup is good, will, in turn, define your balance, and (3) the strike and contact with the ball, which is necessarily determined in large part by the two previous elements but which also involves significant specific skill in the coordination of the hands.

Professional and elite amateur golfers refine their swings much more minutely than I think the average golfer should. Therefore, they focus on more than just these three broad elements. If you're that good and playing competitive golf, then more specific work with a high-speed camera might make sense for your practice. The space between the best players in the world is razor-thin, and it's incredibly difficult to improve at that level. Most of us, though, are missing the forest for the trees by focusing our practice the way Rickie Fowler does. When working on our game, we should instead assess those three core essential elements broadly and figure out where issues are creating persistent problems or inconsistencies. Then, with that knowledge, we can develop feedback heuristics to teach ourselves to fix those issues. This process of evaluating and improving, repeated judiciously, will produce an improved swing and, eventually, a good one.

THE BACKSWING

The first motion in a golf swing is to pick the club off the ground and draw it back behind your body to prepare to strike the ball. In the annals of golf history, there have been numerous successful approaches to this movement. Even in a single player, the backswing will change for shot-making needs. For instance, most players will shorten their backswing to hit a low penetrating shot in windy conditions. When I want to hit it up in the air, I draw the club back even farther than normal. These variations are, indeed, nearly infinite.

Because of all this, my opinion is that there isn't a universally correct approach to the backswing. I've watched players like Rory McIlroy, Tiger Woods, and Ben Hogan do it with aching grace. On the other hand, Hideki Matsuyama, Jim Furyk, and Arnold Palmer all achieved great success with homemade approaches. This, combined with my opinion that the swinging motion is a natural human movement, suggests to me this piece of advice: when learning to swing or trying to improve a swing, it's better to focus on the essential elements of that backswing, getting those really right, than it is to attempt to emulate some ideal backswing prototype. Once you know what's important, let your natural physiology and athletic ability do the rest. The essential elements of a backswing that cannot be compromised are weight shift and rotation.

WEIGHT

First, weight. Your backswing has to move the center of your weight behind the ball. Though a large amount of the force in a golf swing is built through rotation, the move always involves a shift of weight forward to help gain momentum to meet the ball. If you don't get this right and your weight is too far back or forward when that forward shift occurs, you will find yourself off balance at and through contact. This makes it almost impossible to consistently square the clubhead at the point of impact.

I like to think of this as using your two feet for the different parts of the swing. As you swing back, your weight moves off center and plants over your back foot, using the ground as a pivot against which your body can twist and develop arc and tension. Then, like a spring uncoiling, your weight shifts onto your front foot and plants there. This facilitates the release and acceleration of all the tension built up in the backswing.

This weight shift can be difficult to see in a golf swing because while a golfer's center of mass moves laterally, the motion is mostly self-contained. It won't necessarily manifest in observable movements unless you look very closely. The rotation you make, on the other hand, is immediately apparent to any observer.

It's helpful to think of an analogue from another sport to better understand what's happening during the golf swing. Consider a major league pitcher throwing a ball; this dynamic is much clearer there. Tim Lincecum pulled his body way back onto his rear leg when he wound up. If his weight didn't shift onto the back leg, he would fall forward before he even began his pitch. He builds up energy through rotation and movement. Then he releases the energy, shifting his weight forward and planting his front leg in the dirt—his new pivot point. If he didn't plant his lead leg hard, he would fall over again, and he would never be able to transfer the massive energy he had built up in his body to the ball. You can go on YouTube and find a video of the plant failing; he spins around and falls to the ground. That wild spin is all the energy that would have gone into the baseball if his foot had been planted correctly.

While Tim Lincecum's pitch is a more dramatic visual example of the weight transfer than a golfer's swing, they're the same movement on a fundamental level. In your backswing, your weight should transfer onto your back foot and over it. This is a stable position from which to start the downswing and gives you the space to get your body back to the ball with a square clubface at impact. From there, your weight transfers forward and into the ground, and you rotate through. The weight should start around 55/45% front foot to back foot, shift to 80% on your back foot, and then move forward until almost 100% of your weight is over your front foot.

You should be able to feel your weight transfer through your swing, but it might take time to develop that sense. If you can't feel the weight transfer yet, consider some key indicators that it has gone wrong. If you find yourself hitting weak little queefy slices and dead pulls, your center of mass may be too far forward when you start your downswing. Rotation is occurring too far forward, with your body ahead of the point of impact. From there, all you can do is try to correct with your hands. And when you can't, you are either trap-pulling it or cutting across the ball and putting a slice spin on it. If you're topping or missing the ball entirely, your weight may have stayed too far back.

A common aberrant weight transfer to avoid is "sway." Many golfers struggle to differentiate the weight transfer described above, which is a shift of the whole body's mass through the feet, from a swaying movement where the upper body moves back over the feet. Golfers often sway because they're not flexible enough to rotate,[41] and, stuck, they move their trunk backward instead. While difficult to feel, this is easily recognized from the side or rear viewing angles. You can see their upper body sway back in their backswing and then sway forward in the downswing.

For some people, this aberrant motion might come from trying to hit the ball too hard.[42] Indeed, when a pronounced sway is timed up well, it might produce some power, but this comes at the cost of great inconsistency. Timing up a swaying upper body along with a golfer's rotation makes getting the clubface back on the ball more difficult. Time it a hair too early or too late, and the center of mass

---

41 We haven't discussed rotation yet, but it's a core component of the full swing.
42 Although as you'll see below, I think there might just be no such thing.

will be behind or ahead of the ball at impact, the hands will have to try to compensate to make contact, and literally any miss is in play.

To correct sway, Harvey Penick, Lee Trevino, and I'm sure many others have said that you should try to keep your head behind the ball at impact. This is often taught by telling golfers to "keep their heads still." While everyone's head must move during the swing, it is true that at impact, a good golfer's head is behind the ball. Despite this, I have found that trying to practice this is too rigid and makes it difficult to move naturally. By all means, try it out, but if you're like me and find yourself feeling stuck while keeping your head still, you can try something else.

I like to think about my rear plant foot as the outer bound of movement and focus on rotating around it. Instead of using my head as the cue, I use my hip. This translates the energy that would go into sway into rotation instead, conveniently correcting the problem and producing more power. Be warned, though, the limiting factor on rotation is likely flexibility, meaning that when you first start attempting this remedy, you may not physically be capable of doing the correct movement through a full swing's range of motion. This is one of many reasons golf cannot be rushed and must be learned over an extended period. Your body needs time to adapt, so practice it little by little until you can achieve a position you're happy with. Just remember not to let your upper body sway.

Unlike most aspects of a golf swing, I think the weight distribution can be felt readily through your feet. To me, this suggests that the weight shift doesn't require special practice techniques to refine.

Some specialized tools, like force pads, are designed to train this, but I think they're a waste of your cash. Buy a bucket of Coronas instead. *La familia* baby.

The essential kernel of understanding that I want you to take away from this is that a transition back over but not past your rear foot is sound. Use this as a cue to guide your practice sessions, and if you notice the flaws associated with poor weight transfer, go back to basics. Make sure your weight is coming back and drill it until it's second nature. Sway can be pernicious and difficult for golfers to perceive in their swing, but this exception proves the rule. When I find myself swaying too much and really get stuck, I like to plant a survey stake on my right side, right up against my body. If I start to sway, I'll hit the stick and feel it. This keeps me from moving my body past my rear leg at all, and I quickly return the energy I had been using to sway into rotation.

Getting this fundamental correct will create a more powerful, easily repeatable swing.

ROTATION

In concert with the weight transfer in the backswing comes a big turn. The amount of rotation varies, from Gary Player's or Bubba Watson's massive windups to Lee Trevino's or Jon Rahm's abbreviated backswings. The specific makeup of a swing depends on the needs and abilities of the golfer. Gary Player is a tiny little guy, and if he didn't swing out of his shoes, he would have no chance of competing. Jon Rahm, on the other hand, has what NFL coaches call a "big bubble" and can sacrifice some distance for the control he gains from an abbreviated swing. Everyone is different, and you will be, too, so you should experiment with it until you find something that feels right. I'll give you a few general principles that can guide you.

Rotation in the golf swing occurs when, in concert, you turn your lead shoulder back toward your back foot and pull your hands behind your back. The top of your lead shoulder will move under your chin while your hips stay relatively level to your target line. This creates torque between your shoulders and hips and builds energy that can be released into the ball later.

Rotation isn't necessarily "natural": you can get your hands to the top of the backswing without actually turning your shoulders very far against your hips. In fact, I think few adults have the flexibility to make a full rotation without growing up in golf or practicing the turn. Despite all this, rotation is fundamental. Swings without turning generate weak shots, so prioritize drilling rotation into your swing. The flexibility you do not have today will come in time, and you will be substantially better for it.

All else being equal, the longer the arc of your clubhead in your backswing, the harder you will be able to hit the ball. My thesis, further fleshed out later in this book, is that hitting the ball harder is better in golf—allowing the large canid to chow, so to speak—so you might want to consider a long arc to build a powerful swing.

There are many different paths to achieve this long arc, each with its benefits and drawbacks. Take Bubba Watson's swing. His shoulders and hands turn away from the ball. His left foot lifts off the ground to allow his hips to rotate too. He comes so far back that even his head turns, and you can see the brim of his hat starting to face backward. The shaft of his club comes behind him, far "past parallel" with the ground. In the 1990s, John Daly famously became the first man to average over 300 yards per drive on tour by taking his club so far past parallel that he could see it out of his left eye at the end of his backswing.

These players use long swings to create long arcs; the clubhead is moving farther away from the golf ball, facilitated by greater rotation of the shoulders and a turn of the hips. These swings are considered durable, with practitioners like Phil Mickelson and Davis Love III continuing to bomb the ball well into middle age without much injury load. The downside, however, is that they're often at least a little bit wild. Big long swings give a lot of room for error, and big lefties Phil and Bubba have hit the wrong fairway enough times to attest to this.

There is another approach to generate a long arc and massive power without going past parallel, maximizing the distance of the hands from a golfer's center of mass. Rather than move the golf club farther behind the player, players using this approach create length by keeping their arms stock straight, pushing their hands farther away and higher from their bodies. This, effectively, creates a long swing without having to go past parallel and entertain all the unpredictability that comes with it. Golfers who use this athletic swing style include (young pre–Hank Haney) Tiger Woods, Rory McIlroy, and Dustin Johnson. This swing style takes enormous flexibility in the hips, torso, shoulders, and wrists and can produce correspondingly enormous power. This also produces the appearance that a golfer is swinging "hard." The downside of this kind of swing is that it puts a lot of torque on the body and is often associated with a greater incidence of injury.

We will never know whether this swing, the (alleged) steroids, or the hookers ruined Tiger's body for good, but proceed with caution if you hope to emulate him here.

While either of these long-swing models produces a full turn, it's also possible to produce what feels like a long arc without completing the body rotation. This is bad, and you should seek to avoid this in your practice. This aberration occurs when a golfer "picks up" the clubhead during the swing, disconnecting the arms from the body and moving them above your body. This might get the club into a position that looks roughly similar to that of a strong golfer. But decoupling that from body rotation will generate little to no torque, produce less power, and make timing more difficult. More likely than not, a golfer picking the club up like this won't get the club into the correct position at the top of the backswing anyway and will end up swinging through the ball either over or under plane, creating any kind of miss (including one of the ball itself).

Some players practice with a towel under their dominant armpit to stay "connected" and prevent the arms from flying away during the swing. I think this is a little weird, although it might be a good cue to the mind to approximate a correct swing. The arms have to move free a little bit in full swing to allow you to get into the right position. So I don't think you want to practice with a towel under your arm all the time, but doing this drill a few times if you find yourself picking up the club will help you learn the feel of a correct connection between your body and arms.

As I noted, all amateur golfers should understand that flexibility is almost always a barrier to correctly executing a top-shelf golf swing. For anyone but highly experienced golfers with well-built swings, it will be difficult to emulate the long, smooth backswings of the professionals I have mentioned above. In addition to this, as we get older, our bodies grow stiff, further compounding the issue. Because of this, I think any good golfer can benefit from a stretching regimen. Your range of motion in the golf swing can be improved with diligent effort, and this increased range of motion will allow you to put your body into advantageous positions during the golf swing. For a novice golfer, hitting balls itself will likely improve your range of motion and flexibility. As a player advances, though, I recommend implementing some well-thought-out stretches.[43]

To help myself limber up before a round, I will take my two iron and put one hand on the grip and the other on the head, then extend my arms out completely in front of me. I'll lower my arms and touch the ground without bending my knees several times, and then in a golf stance, rotate my body as far as I can back and as far as I can through, first with the club straight out in front of me and then

---

43 I do yoga, as well, which I can't recommend emphatically enough. This practice will help you with the mindfulness that I advocate for later in this book as well.

along an approximation of the swing path. I can feel the stretch in my shoulders, lats, and hips as I do this. I'll repeat this several times until I'm nice and loosey-goosey before a round. During a practice session, I push myself to hold the stretch farther and longer than I did in the past. I am no expert on stretching, and I'm sure you or someone with knowledge of anatomy could design an even better routine for you to limber up in key areas. However you do it, stretching will allow you to develop a longer, and therefore more powerful, swing.

A NOTE ON POWER

I think you should swing hard. I said above that I don't think the phrase "You're swinging too hard" means very much, and it's true. When an old-timer tells you you're swinging too hard, much like saying you "picked your head up," they see that your sequencing is off. Many casual observers simply lack the vocabulary to identify "sequencing" as a real issue. In the literal sense, though, I think you should swing hard. This means, in my view, that any golfer learning or trying to improve should aim to move the club at least 80% of the absolute maximum speed they're capable of on every full swing. This is not your hardest swing, but it is swinging hard.

Golf teachings vary on this point. Some instructors will tell you to figure out how to hit the ball straight first, then you can build power. Others will give you the rip stick and let you slap it all over the track, then try to straighten you out later. I say tee it high and let it fly. First, this is important because babying the ball around the golf course is lame, and I don't want you to play that way. Second, I think it's very possible to take a wild bomber and teach them, if not perfect accuracy off the tee, at least to play strategic golf that puts them in a scoring position. On the other hand, I have seen many players who learned to restrain their swings early, hit the ball straight but soft at the start, and then were never able to let loose. Something about that formative experience of swinging softly breaks a golfer's brain; many of them will never learn to play with power.

Golf is a game of power. Some great golfers have lacked it, and some of them have beaten me, but on balance, it's much better to hit the ball hard. More than this, for inexperienced golfers who nonetheless already know how to swing, I think the advice to "not swing so hard" is deadly. As stated above, the golf swing is mostly unfathomable, relying on a complex chain reaction across the golfer's entire body. The only way to do it is with a certain degree of intuition. Trying to take a swing that's flawed but built on this sequencing nonetheless and just telling the poor rube to "slow it down" is sure to mess up that intuition. Even worse, this inexperienced golfer receiving advice might internalize it and start to practice swinging slowly, building a less powerful swing without correcting whatever fault was plaguing them in the first place.

My advice to an inexperienced golfer (and, indeed, this could apply to anyone) is when facing persistent swing issues in a round, rather than trying to fix something that isn't working on-course, strategize around whatever error you are seeing most often. Aim somewhere different. Hit different shots. Whatever you can do to take the part of your game that is killing you out and allow yourself to move the ball toward the hole. Then, when you have time to practice, take a video of your swings and figure out, by yourself or with a teacher, what the actual problem in your swing was. Now understanding the issue, you can work on actually fixing it. Never try to slow your swing down for its own sake. That is moving backward, and this game is hard enough as it is.

SHORT SWINGS

After everything I just told you, I would be remiss if I didn't mention short swings. Power is very important, but the truth is some golfers thrive by shortening their backswing to even less than parallel. I've mentioned Jon Rahm, and Tony Finau is another example. These players wager that the added control of a short swing will compensate for the loss in the distance, and clearly, as some of the best in the world, they are right. One thing to note about these players, though, is that they're usually far more powerful than average, even with these short swings. Players at the far end of the bell curve on natural power can get away with more than you or I can. However, if you build a powerful swing and then want to rein it in, I think more power to you. I would still advocate that new players at least try to build a long swing. Odds are you're not going to have the surplus power of Jon Rahm or Tony Finau, and you can always shorten your swing down the road.

There are also, of course, some people who, because of injury or age, are physiologically incapable of a long swing. While I advocate for long and hard swings, the reality is that it means different things for different people with different capabilities. You will in no way be prevented from playing great golf just because you can't get the club back to parallel. If you can't hit the ball particularly far on your best day, know that Zach Johnson won two majors and hasn't sniffed 300 yards in his life. Power can be an important component of great golf, but great golf comes in many forms and is possible with little to no power at all. Players who lack power will just have to compensate with accuracy and a short game.

THE PLANE

I've talked a little bit about the theoretical pane of glass defining your alignment. There is another pane that Ben Hogan wrote about in his *Five Lessons*. This is the idea of the swing plane. An even swing plane means that the angle of your club to the ground is roughly the same on your backswing as it is on your downswing, thereby staying aligned with Hogan's pane of glass. Even Hogan would admit that all swings vary from the platonic ideal, at least a little bit.[44]

To better understand this concept, think of a kind of slot that the club can fit in at the top of your swing to facilitate good ball-striking. Swinging in this slot has been a path to solid ball-striking for golfers

---

[44] Except, perhaps, Moe Norman's famous one-piece swing. Moe gained consistency by sacrificing power, though, and never won on the PGA tour.

like Tiger Woods, Collin Morikawa, and Brooks Koepka. Swings that remain very on plane are also, it should be said, very beautiful. If your body lends itself to a naturally on-plane swing, I believe that's commendable and will likely serve you well.

On the other hand, I don't think it's actually necessary to be on plane during most of the backswing. At the top of Bubba Watson's backswing, his club crosses way over the plane, and he hits a golf ball as well as anyone around today. Because of this, I don't think being "on plane" should always be a central concern when trying to improve your swing.

Plane issues are usually described in terms relative to the platonic ideal. When the club crosses over the swing plane, usually leading to a chop down on the ball in the follow-through, that is known as "coming over the top." When the club is below the platonic swing plane, that is called being shallow. This vocabulary helps us understand some persistent mistakes that come up in most golfers' swings. Indeed, I have seen people with dramatic plane issues coming in over the top or steep or low and shallow. They probably would benefit from training designed to correct those issues. If you struggle with ball-striking and can't figure out what's wrong, trying to get the shaft more closely aligned with this imaginary plane is a good tool in your remediation toolbox. However, I still want to emphasize that I don't think you need to be fanatical about the swing plane to play good golf. The on-plane swing is just a rough biomechanical proxy for the appropriate place for a backswing. Our physiologies differ, so don't sweat it if a backswing that works for you doesn't look like Ben Hogan.

On the other hand, in the downswing, there is much less space for variation, and maintaining your plane is a central component of all striking. It is often said correctly that PGA players' swings all look different going back but identical at impact. The strike is discussed in more fulsome detail a little later in this book.

As a final takeaway, I hope that you leave this section on the swing plane understanding that your club can't be just anywhere at the top of your backswing, but it can be in a range of places. You can be slightly over the top, shallow, or vertical, fall back into plane on the downswing, and make a good strike. Understand the swing plane, but understand its limits as well.

TIMING

So now you should have an idea of how to start your swing correctly. You want to take the club back behind you on a long arc, creating space for a powerful downswing and building tension in the body. You're moving your weight behind the ball and rotating your upper body against your lower body. In this position, you're ready to uncoil and strike. To execute the next portion of the swing correctly, a golfer must master timing.

This book describes the swing in ordinal sequence, first setup, then the backswing, now timing, and next, the strike. All these elements of a golf swing are intertwined, and all must be fundamentally sound in that order to play consistent golf. If your backswing is wild and unpredictable, you can never build solid timing and make predictable strikes.

Timing is rhythmic. Good timing will make your swing feel effortless yet launch the ball deep down the fairway. Poor timing will feel unbalanced and ungainly and produce chunks, thins, pulls, and shanks. Many of the flaws traditionally pointed out on driving ranges, like "pulling your head" or "swinging too hard," flow from poor timing.

To build good timing in your swing, you first need a fundamental understanding of what is happening in a downswing and how it produces a rhythmic repeatable move. Next, timing takes serious long-term practice. Finally, it requires mental calm.

As I've emphasized, your conscious mind cannot swing a golf club. Mental calm prevents the intrusion of your conscious mind into your swing and allows the automatic parts of your brain to do their work. Don't forget, though, your unconscious mind can't swing a club without training; that's where the knowledge and practice parts come in. Let's start with knowledge.

WHAT IS TIMING?

Timing in music is simple. You hear a beat, one and two and three and four, and naturally synchronize your body to it. The golf swing is rhythmic; it is just two beats, first back, then through. While the underlying motion of your body is far more complex than the beat, a solid feel for rhythm will improve your ball-striking. That feel, however, can't be fully developed until the core mechanics that allow a swing to take place have been mastered.

Timing is facilitated first by sequencing. Consider the downswing in the abstract: first, the feet move; then energy is transferred and amplified by the ankles, knees, hips; and finally, shoulders and arms move until the clubhead is cracking like a whip.

Beginners have varying degrees of feel for this, depending, I think, on their experience with other sports that include analogous weight transfer and twisting motion to the golf swing.

Hockey players, I have noticed, are often good ball-strikers intuitively because the strike of a puck mimics this action. Baseball players, on the other hand, always suck. There is something about the baseball or softball swing that is close enough to a golf swing to recruit the same motor neurons yet dissimilar enough to train them away from effective golf movements. That dooms these athletes on the golf course.[45]

Other new players, who don't even have these analogous experiences, initially look helpless over the ball. You can see them flail when they start, trying to use their arms, unable to build momen-

---

45 When I was nineteen, I was working at a golf course during the day and playing regularly in the afternoon. My caddy, Chet, invited me to join his men's softball league, and I did, for the beer if nothing else. I played the first game and took maybe three at bats, but those few baseball-style swings were enough to screw up my golf swing for the rest of the summer. I would love to tell you that it's fine to play softball if you want to be a good golfer. But in my experience, the two are incompatible. Pitching, on the other hand, translates nicely into the golf swing.

tum through a kinetic chain. If this is you, don't despair. It may just take you a little longer to learn the movements.

One point worth emphasizing here is if you don't have a background in golf, you should feel no embarrassment at all about not being able to hit the ball. I've seen so many people go to the range for the first time and become frustrated because they can't make contact, get the ball off the turf, or hit it very far or straight. If you're a beginner, you shouldn't be able to do these things because you don't yet know how. Hitting a golf ball requires throwing a chunk of metal on the end of a stick at the ground with as much force as possible while maintaining absolute pinpoint accuracy such that that ball then travels consistently to a location you intend and lands in a five-yard-radius circle. To strike the ball requires practice, lots of it. Expect nothing less. Don't be disappointed or frustrated when it doesn't come easily. That's the reality of this game, not a personal failing on your part.

THE MECHANICS OF TIMING

To learn to time your downswing and, in turn, to hit the ball, start with your feet. At the top of the backswing, if you listened to my advice above, your weight should be firmly over your back leg, your torso rotated backward, and your arms in the air behind you. In this position, you're ready to make your move.

Shift your weight forward onto your front foot.

Just that little move, off the back and onto the front, will set in motion a cascade of effects that end in you striking the ball. This shift is accompanied by a slight dip of your weight, facilitating its motion forward and a small further bend in your knees. With this, your hips slide slightly forward and turn against your lead foot. That foot is your pivot; it should be stuck firmly in the ground.

Notice that all this action has occurred, but nothing above your waistline has moved at all yet. Of course, your body is all connected. It would be absurd to attempt to keep your upper body completely still through this process. But if you watch a good golfer do this in slow motion, you will see that the sequencing is clear and consistent, your hips clear first, followed by your upper body and hands moving through the hitting zone.

This brings us to the piece of bad advice described above that pretty much everyone has heard on the range at some point. *Stop swinging so hard.* Golf clubs are meant to be swung hard. Some people, however, observe that poor swings *look* like they're done with excessive force.

The answer, I think, is an error in sequencing. Instead of making a hard transition and rotating the hips through the swing, many golfers, trying to hit the ball harder, will allow their upper body movement to get ahead of their lower body. If your arms are moving out of turn, they will start doing the work of moving the club themselves, and your arms are weak as shit compared with your legs.[46] This throwing of arms and upper body gives the appearance of great effort, hence the "swinging too hard" edict. More than this, because the player has rotated back but not allowed their body to follow proper sequencing to return to the front, they will be too far back when they throw their club at the ball. This will result in a combination of thin, weak line drives and fat chunks. If someone says you're swinging too hard, think sequencing and balance and refer back here.

LARRY BIRD DRILL

As a player, I have struggled mightily with moving my upper body too early and getting ahead of my legs in the golf swing. The way I eventually taught myself to resolve this problem, and what I advocate for other golfers trying to improve or learn, is to start to feel the rhythm with a half or partial swing. With so many moving parts in the full swing, it can be difficult to isolate the lower body in your mind to train it to fix bad timing. Instead, I like to draw the club back only a short distance and start swinging from there. I call this the Larry Bird drill.

When Larry Bird practiced shooting, he didn't start with deep threes. Instead, he worked in to out, starting with shots very close

---

46 There's a story I remember hearing once of some reporter going to lift weights with Roger Clemens during the peak of baseball's steroid era. The reporter, seeing Clemens's robust upper body, commented that "with arms like that it must be easy to throw the ball hard." Clemens gave him a hard look and said, "No, it's all legs." Golf is the same. Don't skip leg day if you want to hit the ball farther.

to the basket and gradually taking longer ones until his body was coordinated. You should do the same. Start by taking the clubhead just to knee height. At the "top" of this backswing, shift your weight, rotate your hips, and let that pull the clubhead through the ball. This feels really awkward at first, and I hit many shanks trying to break the swing down like this. But once you get the feel and your legs and hips start doing the work, you will find yourself hitting straight, hard chip shots onto the range.

This is a good teaching aid because you have no way to throw your hands and arms at the ball from this ergonomically disadvantageous position. If you want to hit it at all, you have to use your legs. The secret is that this is true of the golf swing as a whole, but you have to start small to trick your brain into actually doing it.

You are ready to level up when you can repeat this drill consistently, making good contact no fewer than seven or eight times in ten. Now, you can move your club back to a half swing. In the half swing, your hands reach roughly parallel to your belt buckle or slightly higher. The club should now be well off the turf and pointing away from the ground, although the exact angle is not essential at this stage. From here, you can execute a real shot, and you could, if you so choose, start to use your hands and arms to make your shot. Resist this temptation; apply what you learned with the dinky little knee-high shots. Get your hands to the top of your new backswing and use your lower body to turn yourself back into the shot. If you find yourself messing up and throwing your hands repeatedly, go back to the knee-high shots. You aren't ready for this smoke yet. Apply the same technique through practice here; you should be sending straight, consistent shots down the range. You're ready to advance when you can do this seven or eight times in ten again.

The next swing length is three-quarters. Here, your club's shaft should come roughly parallel to your chest or a little past it. This is not a full swing, but it nearly is. Some golfers prefer to take all their iron shots this way, judging that the increase in control on the flight of the ball makes up for the loss of maximum distance.[47]

Your wrists should be cocked for the three-quarter swing to get the club behind you and create lag. From there, you can use your hands, once you learn the skill (detailed below, to some degree, in the strike section), to manipulate the trajectory and spin of your golf ball. You can also use your hands to correct errors.

To continue to develop your swing here, apply the same Larry Bird technique you have learned from knee-high and half swings. Work with your legs and hips until you're hitting good shots.

After you master three-quarter swings, the final boss is the full swing. If you've followed my technique so far and are hitting consistently good shots with your three-quarter swings, your golf game is

---

[47] I think a lot of golfers' preferences in swing can be attributed to the conditions in the places where they learned. In Scotland and West Texas, where there's limited tree cover and wind plays a major role in the flight of the ball more or less all the time, players tend to have shorter swings built to emphasize lower ball flight. Where I grew up in Maine, fairways were lined with tall trees. If you hit the ball off-line, you had to be able to launch the ball up high in the air to get over them. The wind also was blocked by all this foliage, facilitating high ball flights. Consequently, I learned a long swing that hits the ball very high, and it has taken me much effort to play links golf effectively.

LET THE BIG DOG EAT

likely in pretty good shape. Advancing to full swings will just help you hit the ball a little farther and perhaps higher.

At the top of the full swing, the club should be somewhere near parallel to the ground. Some people prefer less than parallel; I like to swing past parallel. You may want to use the physical boundary of your own flexibility to time up the top of your backswing. But if you use the margin of your physical ability as a timing device, then early in the morning or when it's cold, conditions in which you feel tight, your timing may be thrown off. For this reason, I would advocate having your full swing be somewhere less than your body's most capable rotation.

To drill your full swing, apply the techniques from above and try to get some good shots off.

LOUIS OOSTHUIZEN

Like the other aspects of the swing, timing can't be the product of intuition alone. It has to be learned through careful practice. I can't tell you how to time up your swing, and if I was standing with you on the range, I couldn't show you. You have to learn to feel it within yourself. That's the power of the Larry Bird drill; you feel your way into a repeatable tempo through repetition and then let that guide you.

I think in this area, it's also helpful to just watch great players swing. Some part of their rhythm gets into you when you see their swings. While it might not feel as effortless for you as it looks for them, some of their magic can't help but get into you. Watching the Masters in 2021, Ian Baker-Finch marveled at Louis Oosthuizen's swing. Louis isn't a big man and doesn't appear to be swinging very hard at all, yet he hits the ball far farther than he has any business doing. "If you're watching at home, kids," Baker-Finch said, "just say Louis in your backswing, and Louis as you swing through, *Louis-Louis*." Watch Louis play, and you'll see that he has that perfectly sequenced timing from his backswing into his transition.

Watch Louis swing, and get the feel inside you, then go out and say *Louis-Louis* in your head to feel the tempo and backswing, then follow-through. Repeat this fifty times on the range with a seven iron; you'll start to find your own tempo. Once you have a feel for it, you can practice it more and more until it becomes second nature.

I remember being a kid watching the British Open in the summer in this little basement room at my local golf course. When I couldn't stand it anymore, I'd run out on the course to replicate what I saw. I always swung better on those days. You will too.

FINAL NOTE ON TIMING

On timing, I'll leave you with this: the most important thing about tempo, in your own practice, is knowing what is actually caused by your tempo and what isn't. If your fundamentals are not dialed in, it'll be really hard to tell what issues come from tempo and what don't.

Sometimes my feel for shotmaking is just screwed up, and in those times, the best solution is to do the Larry Bird drill and get my swing back into rhythm. Just as often, though, something in my setup or backswing is putting me in such a disadvantageous position to the ball that I have to overcompensate on the downswing, and I'm thereby putting myself out of sequence. This feels like an issue in timing, but you have to remember that problems with your setup and backswing will very rarely *feel* wrong. If they did, you wouldn't be doing them incorrectly. Your setup and backswing feel right when they do what you're comfortable with. But when you feel comfortable with poor fundamentals, you will feel good swinging but produce bad shots.

This phenomenon might lead you to feel like your tempo is off. Someone might start telling you that you're swinging too hard or pulling your head. Really, though, many of your issues will likely start with fundamentals first. This is why you have to drill those aspects of the swing to be technically right first. By doing that hard analytic work, using objective tools like a surveying stake and a camera, you are teaching yourself to feel comfortable when your body is in a good golf position. Then, you can work on getting the tempo right.

How can you tell the difference? Rely on the same analytic tools. Make sure that you're aligned, and video your swing. If you've watched a reasonable amount of golf, you should be able to see where you're out of position in the backswing. If everything looks good and you aren't hitting your best shots, *Louis-Louis*, it's time to go to tempo town.

THE STRIKE

The strike is the moment the clubhead makes contact with the ball. For all the effort that goes into the rest of the golf swing, the strike is all that matters on a fundamental level. The golf ball will be in contact with the club for only milliseconds, and everything that happens afterward will be defined by that briefest moment. There are several variables that great golfers can manipulate to achieve desired contact in that moment. These are, at least, face angle, swing path, angle of attack, and point of contact—all of which are described below.

The golf swing elements build iteratively: first setup, then backswing, then swing tempo. This order gives you time to build underlying fundamentals before practicing the more complicated parts of the golf swing. Training of the actual golf ball strike can't be delayed in the same way, though. I mean, let's face it; you can't really practice golf without the strike being a major component of your experience. Plant as many surveying sticks in the ground as you want. You're not getting anywhere if you're not putting the clubhead on the ball. Despite this, I think there are a few good reasons to leave the strike for last.

First, if you're a novice or intermediate golfer who has trouble making consistent contact, your best training for striking the ball better is probably just going out, working the areas of the swing I described above, and getting reps putting the clubhead onto the golf ball. There is a neuromuscular refinement and coordination to hitting a golf ball that I think can be learned only by repeated, sometimes even tedious, practice. I'm sorry, but you will not consistently hit the ball well in your first thousand swings. You probably won't in the next thousand, either. Given that reality, the best course for a lot of you is just to go out, think about setup, think about backswing, think about tempo, and get that clubhead on the ball a lot of times until your body has learned how to do that.

The second reason the strike is last here is that for the advanced golfer, it can be among the most intricate parts of the game. Advanced players can use their hands and arms to manipulate the clubhead at impact and create an array of wonderful shots. High hooks, low-slinging slices, dead balls, and spinners. These are all manipulated to some degree in the milliseconds before your club-head hits the ball. Unfortunately, these delicate arm and hand corrections happen too fast to enter the consciousness, much less be fully understood. Refining the strike to create repeatable draws, fades, and high and low balls are damn near witchcraft. If you're not solid on your setup, backswing, and timing, you probably shouldn't even try.

That being said, good golfers should understand the strike. There are a few key elements of the strike that everyone should think about all the time, too, so we start there.

ELEMENTS OF THE STRIKE

Face Angle

The first key element of the strike is face angle, the direction the clubhead is facing when it strikes the ball. Research using Trackman swing-tracking radar equipment has shown that the direction the golf ball travels after the strike is defined mostly by the direction of the clubface at the time of impact. This is called face angle.

Swing Path

The second primary factor in ball flight is the swing path. The swing path is the direction the club is traveling when it strikes the ball. Just as the face angle dictates the direction the ball will start, the direction the club is moving is essential to the movement of the ball. The ball's spin is defined by the angle between the face angle and the direction the club is moving. That spin will change the ball's path in the air, creating draws, hooks, cuts, and slices.

Angle of Attack

The third element of the strike is the angle of attack of the golf club. The angle of attack defines how steeply the clubhead is descending toward the ball. The degrees of loft of the golf club minus this angle of attack[48] produces the "dynamic loft" of the clubface at impact. By changing the dynamic loft of the golf club, the angle of attack will

---

48 Technically, the angle of attack is added, not subtracted. Because the club should be on a downward path for all clubs but the driver, the angle of attack is generally negative, hence the subtractive quality.

LET THE BIG DOG EAT

determine a number of characteristics of the ball's flight.[49] In particular, the angle of attack is extremely important to the ball's launch trajectory and backspin. Depending on wind conditions, these changes could buoy the ball farther up to float in the air or penetrate through it. Spin imparted by the strike will also affect what the ball does when it lands on the green. Top spin will make it rocket forward, while modest backspin may cause it to take one hop and stop. Strong backspin can even suck it off the front of the green.

Location of the Strike

The fourth element of the strike, and the final one mentioned here, is the location of the strike on the clubface. Balls hit close to the center of the clubface will transfer more of the energy from your swing into the ball, producing harder-hit balls that fly closer to the direction of the clubhead. Balls hit outside the center of the face will be weaker and may move in odd directions. Balls hit far out to the margin of the clubface have a habit of shooting off to the side and scaring your playing partners, which can be embarrassing or hilarious, depending on your perspective. These are called shanks or hosel rockets, and we all hit them, so don't be ashamed. While they rarely show it on TV, even PGA pros hit shanks.

That's a lot going on just from contact! The good news is that 90% of it can be simplified for most golfers. Even some very skilled golfers

---

49 Because the golf club hits the ball from a downward angle, the angle of attack will generally reduce the dynamic loft to something less than the static loft of the club lying flat at address. The exception to this is the driver, which is ideally hit at a slightly upward angle, increasing the club's dynamic loft and producing high, low-spinning shots.

would probably benefit from simplifying a lot of their ball-striking. My broader theory here is discussed further in the strategy section below. Good golf is consistent golf, and trying to manipulate the elements of the strike described above will always add variables and, thus, inconsistency to your game. Many players, PGA pros, great PGA pros, basically play the same shot all the time. They focus on drilling all those factors to be consistent and to hit the ball well every time rather than trying to manipulate them to get fancy.

Not everyone has this approach, and having fun with your shots is important too. Some players like Bubba and Tiger have had great success manipulating the ball wildly. Just know that the more you do this, the more variability you introduce into your game. Understanding what is happening in your strike is good to produce different trajectories or spins on the ball. But fundamentally, simplicity is better when you can get away with it.

SWING THROUGH THE BALL

While the strike itself is just milliseconds of contact, the concept of swinging through the ball is so closely related that I think they should be discussed together. Failing to swing through the ball is probably the biggest problem I see in inexperienced golfers at the range. This fault dramatically impairs many high- to mid-handicap golfers even more than funky swing paths.

I've seen so many variations of this. Some people hack down at the ball and appear to be trying to stop the club at the point of contact. Others slap at the ball like it spilled a drink on them. Still others seem nervous and lose steam near the bottom of the club path. I've seen players make these woeful moves only to pull the club up behind their head, attempting to imitate the finish of Tiger or Rory.

Swinging through the ball, generally, means allowing the clubhead to keep moving or even accelerating past the strike and into the follow-through.

Your body cannot make a good strike at the golf ball without swinging through it. Emphasizing a swing that continues through the ball or even feels like it's accelerating through is one of the best tools you have available to ensure that you make clean, crispy strikes.

For some reason, when certain players think too much during their swing, they try to hit at the ball. This has the effect of actually slowing the swing down. To feel like you're hitting at the ball, your body actually has to decelerate the club before it makes contact. To maintain maximum speed through contact, the club has to swing without decelerating at all. This is why powerful swings feel like they're moving through the ball, not at the ball, even though the actual relevant contact occurs only at the instant of the strike.

Luckily, swinging through the ball is a natural motion. While you may instinctively attempt to hit at the ball, if you know how to throw a baseball or skip a stone, you fundamentally understand the sensation of swinging through it. Just let your arms and the clubhead pass through the contact zone and freely up around you. If you fail to do so, it's because you exert effort against the club.

The fact is, your body has no idea how to hit a ball, but it knows how to throw or swing. And to hit a ball well, you just have to swing and let the ball get in the way. In our minds, the process can sometimes adopt more grandeur and seem more refined than this, but this is really what's happening. A swing with any power at all will move the club through the ball, and then your body will guide it up over your shoulders. The club ends up high above the shoulders of good golfers in the follow-through because the energy of the swing has to dissipate. If the club kept moving forward, the golfer would fall on their back.

It may look like pro golfers are pulling the clubs up into that beautiful finish, but rest assured, the clubs are pulling them. If your club isn't pulling you somewhere after you hit the ball, you're probably decelerating the clubhead and should work on swinging through the ball. Lucky you, I got drills.

Try this when you find yourself failing to swing through the ball or decelerating. Tee up the ball on the practice range, and put a tee in front and to the outside (i.e., to the right, for a right-handed golfer) of your golf ball into the ground. Through your strike of the golf ball, focus on throwing the club head out toward the tee placed in front of you. You should feel the club pulling you forward as you make this move, and you should translate that energy naturally around your body. This drill is simple, but it will be apparent immediately if you're not swinging out and through the ball (i.e., from the inside).

Swinging through the ball is crucial to playing effective golf. Multiple successful backswings, grips, and setups exist, but all PGA players look virtually the same at impact. When I started doing the drill above, even now, if I try to practice it, I hit a ton of shanks and feel like it isn't working. You will probably feel uncomfortable at first when you do this drill or any of the drills I prescribe. Remember, though, comfort isn't your friend. The swing you're comfortable with is the one hitting the ball badly, after all. Keep practicing the swing out until your hands and body learn to put the clubhead back on the ball. You will become a more consistent, more powerful ball-striker.

You can also practice this feel using a weighted club, which will help the clubhead swing out in front of you as is correct. As a kid, I would hold two or three clubs together to simulate this effect and make big, loose swings. While this is useful for getting a feel for swinging through the ball, I think most of your practice should consist of actually hitting a ball. Remember, much of golf is learning the fine motor coordination in your hands and wrists to actually put the center of that clubhead on that little white ball.

SPIN AND TRAJECTORY

Golfers use spin in two ways. First, the mindful way: great golfers keep spin in mind for every shot to ensure that their ball falls the right way out of the air and will do what they want on the green. Second, the fun way: golfers put huge amounts of spin on the ball to bend its flight to their will. This creates soaring hooks and banana slices like Bubba.

The former approach to spin is a crux of the game and of the golfer's swing. Every variable together will coalesce into spin and trajectory, and only golfers in control of themselves will be able to consistently command the ball.

The latter approach, on the other hand, is a little reckless. You might learn fairly quickly how to get the ball to bend one way or the other, pop up in the air, or run low. However, playing these shots is far too unpredictable and difficult for most golfers to execute consistently. I have hit many more terrible shots trying to do something cool than I have pulled off the spectacular shot around an obstacle. But man, when you get it just right, it is one of the most incredible feelings.

I think this kind of "shotmaking" is worthwhile for two reasons. First, practicing this skill and trying to make extraordinary shots will refine the skills for the ordinary everyday spin control that ultimately levels up your game. Second, it's hella fun, hoss. That counts.

I was seventeen, in competition, with a line of trees to my right and between me and the green. I was too close to the trees to go over them and had no line to the hole underneath. So I figured the only way to make par was to hit the ball out to the left and put so much cut spin on it that it came back across the tree line. I made that shot, landing it a few paces short of the front of the green. Then I made the up and down for par and went on to win the tournament. That shot was dumb as hell. Going out to the left brought massive trouble into play that would, on average, outweigh the stroke I likely gained by going over the trees. The smart play in these situations is almost always to chip back into the fairway and live to see another day.

But I don't remember any stories from when I was seventeen and chipping out into the fairway, do I?

SPIN

Spin is really fun to play with, and golf is a game, after all. It's worth learning to uncork spin when you really need it or when you just really want to, and scores be damned. As I said, you will always be playing with some spin, so even if you don't want to play the game of hitting hooks and slices on command, it's helpful to have a feel for how your swing changes affect the spin of the ball.

It's also important to know that you will find weird spins cropping up in your game for no reason at all. Some people beat themselves up over this and think some core flaw in their swing needs to be fixed. In my view, most random flaws that pop up in your swing are just the result of natural variation. Most of the mistakes you make just happen for *no reason at all.*

If you understand how to control your spin, you will have the most powerful tool to correct errant spins the next time you're in this situation. Take whatever errant spin you get and try to do the opposite. This should balance out to a relatively straight shot. Slicing the ball? Hit a draw. Hooking it? Hit a cut. It sounds stupidly, reductively, simple, but in my game and the games of people I have given this advice to, I have seen it repeatedly work wonders. Along with checking your setup, this is a core tool in your on-course toolbox.

Since it's clear that learning how to control spin is valuable, you might be wondering, *how do I do that?* Start with the basics.

If the ball spins away from your body, for a right-handed player to the right or clockwise, the ball will move in the opposite direction of the swing. For a right-handed player, this moves the ball to the right. This is called a cut. When the spin is pronounced, it's called a slice—which also happens to be the most common ball flight issue for average golfers. For reasons that people with knowledge of biomechanics and access to tracking software understand, but I do not,[50] cuts tend to lose some amount of distance compared with straight balls and especially draws. Cuts also tend to go higher in the air, making them more susceptible to wind, but then again, they land softer on greens and fairways. Many great players like Jack Nicklaus and Dustin Johnson have primarily played a cut. Players who can get away with this tend to be natural bombers of the ball, like me, who can accept giving up a few yards of distance for what they see as greater control of the ball. There's an old saying that you can talk to a cut, but a hook won't listen, which may or may not be true.

To hit a cut, you have to have your clubface open relative to the path of the club at impact. The direction of your clubface at contact will determine the direction the ball goes, and the angle between that direction and the direction of your swing will determine spin. If

---

50 Might have something to do with the dynamic loft being higher, because the clubhead is relatively more open at impact?

you draw an imaginary line perpendicular to the clubface at impact, and another line representing the path of your club head through the bottom of your swing, when the second line comes from the outside of the first, that will create an "open" clubface and produce a cut.

Note that this is contrary to historical golf teaching and has become commonly known only in the contemporary age of high-speed cameras and tracking software. The old way to teach a cut was just to open the club up at address and aim slightly left. The thinking was that the path of the clubhead determined the initial direction of the ball, and the direction of the face determined the spin or, roughly, where the ball would end up. If you were initially taught this way, know that it's backward. Suppose it does work (which it may, to be honest); in that case, it's probably because that setup is priming you to make some contortions to your body to promote that flight.

A draw, on the other hand, is a ball that spins in the same direction of the swing toward your body, and a hook is just a big draw. To hit a draw, you have to have your clubface closed relative to the path of the club at impact. While cuts come from swinging from the outside, draws come from swinging from the inside. For the right-handed player, these balls move to the left.

Draws, as the evil step-twin of cuts, tend to go significantly farther than the straight ball and often have a lower trajectory, again for reasons I don't pretend to fully understand.

Draws are less susceptible than cuts to high winds—you're unlikely to see the sad floaters with this spin. That said, they're not necessarily a good antidote to windy conditions. Wind will amplify any spin on the ball and can have some very wacky outcomes, including sometimes finding your tight little draw two fairways over. Draws come out lower, which means they often are less forgiving on the greens and can come in a little hot and skip through tight greens if landed too deep. Draws are favored by great players who were trying to maximize their distance when they learned to play, like Rory McIlroy and Cam Smith. They may make sense for you if you're trying to get enough distance to be competitive.[51] Fun fact: I hit lots and lots and lots of shanks trying to learn how to draw the ball, but it all worked out, and now I can teach you.

The first step to learning to hit cuts and draws is just standing up to the ball and trying to do it. I know this sounds stupid, but it's true. There is no mechanical secret to controlling the spin; you just do it. I remember reading Tiger's book when I was a kid. His advice was basically, "Listen, if I want to hit the ball with spin, I just think about what spin I want before I swing, and then I do it, but obviously, you can't do that, so here's some advice." To me, the really valuable advice was the first bit because it revealed the secret that every tour pro and every good player who has control over their spin is mostly intuiting it.

When I stand up to the ball and try to hit a cut, I don't think about all the elements of my swing I need to change to cut the ball; I just do it. If we did try to think through the elements of the swing,

---

51 Note that Rory absolutely blisters the ball now and could easily get away with hitting a cut, but he keeps the draw as his stock shot because that's what he's most comfortable with. The best players in the world choose a shot they like best and mostly stick to it; you should do the same thing.

just like I said above, it would be impossible to execute. In fact, thinking about the swing makes us susceptible to pressure. So you wanna learn to control your spin—the first step is just to stand up to the ball and try.

Your body will do a bunch of stuff to get the ball to spin, but it must be initiated by your feel. This feeling will always form the basis of shotmaking. To complement it, you should consider the different elements of the swing that you can change to emphasize these shots.

While I would do your initial training from a neutral setup to make it easier to recognize what spin you're putting on the ball relative to your stock shot, once you get into training different spins, you should adjust your setup to accommodate. The amount you want to adjust your feet and alignment will vary with personal preference. I like a dramatic change, but some prefer something more subtle. Either way, your alignment has to consider that the ball will not go straight at your target but come out on one line and move. For cuts, you always want to be aligned to the left of your eventual target. For draws, you always want to be aligned to the right. If you don't do this, you will find yourself missing your targets regularly. From here, many players will adjust the club at address to be slightly open to the target line for a cut or closed to the target line for a draw. I do this sometimes, though I don't think it's truly necessary. Having a club too far open or closed will likely promote extreme mishits (especially under pressure).

The next locus of adjustment is the backswing. For a cut, I like to feel my hands come farther away from my body and higher in my backswing. I imagine Bubba Watson's high loopy swing while I'm swinging and just try to do that. For me, this helps get the clubhead outside a neutral path, promoting an outside strike of the ball and, thus, a cut. It also helps me get a little more length in the backswing, which offsets some of the distance lost from a cut shot.

For a draw, I feel the club come farther inside my natural swing path and feel my torso curl with more turns. This helps me feel like I'm delivering the club from the inside out, which will promote a hard draw. These are just my feels in the backswing. You will have to develop your own to hit these shots consistently. Still, the goal for each must be for a cut to deliver the club from the outside and slightly across the ball and for a draw to deliver it from the inside to the outside of the ball.

Finally, there is voodoo that happens around the strike of the ball. These are, broadly, corrections that you make with your hands, wrists, and forearms to promote your desired shot and correct any issues in your swing up to this point. This game is mostly practice, feel, and hand-eye coordination, but there are some feelings you can emphasize to help learn this too. To hit cuts, most players feel like they're holding off their hands, keeping their dominant wrist open through impact and allowing the clubface to maintain a relatively open angle to the swing path. In the converse, for a draw, players like to feel their hands closing and turning over, which roughly means their dominant hand, the right hand for a right-handed golfer, is turning to the left at the bottom of the swing, closing the club.

Of course, it's not the rotation of the clubhead itself that produces the spin but just the angle between the clubhead and swing path at impact that creates the desired shot. While it feels like you're pulling the ball to the left during a draw, this is just an illusion.

This work with the hands and wrists is one of the hardest aspects of the golf swing to explain or teach, but for good players, it makes up a large part of shotmaking, so just practice it and feel it out until you get the hang of it.[52]

That's as much as I understand about spin. It's harder to impart side spin with a wedge, so I sometimes go to the range and try to hook 50-degree gap wedges as far as possible. I hit cuts with my driver, then I hit draws. Once you get a feel for moving the ball from side to side, base repetition is the best way to refine your technique. There are physical cues to these shots, but I think they're fundamentally less important than feel and practice when it comes to this particular skill. If you wanted more detailed advice than that here, fucking sue me.

To actually play with spin, just remember that the big hooks and slices will always be hard to control. And the smart money is on finding a spin you can play consistently and using it for as many shots as the course will allow. Only when you're forced to deviate from your most comfortable shot should you begin to consider trying to alter your spin. This discipline will be the seed of many great rounds.

---

52 This will take years, at a minimum, I'm afraid.

TRAJECTORY

Now, understanding spin, as best as one can understand spin, it's time to close this discussion on swing mechanics with trajectory.

Trajectory is hugely important. I didn't fully learn this lesson until my late twenties, when I finally had enough money to travel and started playing links courses.[53] The winds ripping across those flatlands tore my scorecards to shreds, and I knew I had to learn to hit it low to survive. Don't be a dummkopf like me; this stuff really matters!

You really want to control your trajectory when it's windy out. You want to hit it high on courses tightly lined or obstructed by trees. When hitting a long drive with the wind at your back, you want to get the ball up in the air to let the wind carry it. When hitting into the fan on an open links track, you want to flight the ball down. When hitting a small green or firm green, you want to drop the ball down from on high to hold it on. You want to keep the ball low beneath the branches when you're playing from the trees after an errant tee shot (as I often find myself doing).

As you can see, there are many, *many* ways that you can use different trajectories to your advantage. Beware, though, as trying to change the trajectory of your shot can introduce its own bevy of

---

53 Links golf is the traditional course design frequently seen in the UK and Ireland. It involves large, mostly treeless courses with firm fairways that tend to let the ball roll for a long time after landing. These courses are relatively exposed to the wind. Compare this with parkland courses more common in the northeastern United States. These courses are heavily tree-lined and often soft, permitting only limited roll.

errors into your ball-striking. As with spin, you want to practice it repeatedly, experiment to identify shots you are comfortable with, and use them to create consistent success on the course.

Your first and most important tool to control your trajectory is club selection. This should be obvious, but I find people are skittish with it. My playing partner will find himself 120 yards out from the green with a low overhanging branch right next to him. When I tell him to pull four iron, I get so many wide-eyed crazy looks.

My basic rule is that clubs with higher loft want to hit the ball higher, and no matter what you do to combat that, they will try to get the ball up in the air. Correspondingly, low-lofted clubs will always tend to hit the ball lower regardless of what you do to compensate.

When you're under a tree, where you are probably three shots from the cup in the best scenario, and the worst possible thing you can do is hit the tree, you must play a club that's least likely to hit the tree—this will be a low-lofted club like a four iron. The other side of that coin is when you're behind a shrub, the lip of a bunker, or whatever, you must take enough loft to get over the obstacle—this will be a high-lofted club like a wedge.

If you're in a fairway bunker up against the lip, chunking the ball 10 yards forward is a bummer, probably a bogey, but with a chance at par. Hitting the ball into the lip, not getting out of the bunker, and possibly putting yourself in a worse position is a disaster. I talk about percentage plays in the strategy section, but you must be mindful of this in the trajectory game. Take the club that you *know* will get you out of trouble and try to get *that club* onto the green every time, rather than pulling the club that you think will be easiest to get onto the green and trying to work it out of trouble.

This understanding of club choice and trajectory has relevance outside scrambling situations. The quickest way to develop a lower ball flight in a stiff breeze is just to take one or two more irons than your stock shot would require, choke down, and shorten your swing. If you have practiced this move, you should produce shots that go the appropriate distance with a lower, more penetrating flight.

This can be taken to wacky extremes. I was playing Cabot Links in Nova Scotia a few years back. The 14th hole is a comically short par 3 pointing out toward the water. On a calm day, this 90-yard shot would be easy, although it's downhill to a small green surrounded by trouble. When we played, it wasn't calm. The first day we played, the wind was whipping. We were all strong golfers, but none of us could get the ball on the green. We finished the round just as the weather was picking up, driving most of the other players off the course. Sensing an opportunity, we decided to go back out to the 14th tee and see if we could get balls onto the green. With that wind coming in, we tried everything: seven iron, short; six iron, short; even a five iron. Nothing could get there. Eventually, from 90 yards out, I chip-cut a three wood that landed on the putting surface. Sometimes the right club seems absurd. Embrace that reality to play good golf.

The second tool at your disposal to control trajectory is your choice of spin. As you will know by now, a cut goes higher and a draw lower than the platonic straight shot.[54] If you open the clubface at impact to get more loft and try to hit the ball higher, you will probably hit cuts, and if you close it to try to hit it lower, you will likely add draw spin. In this way, spin and trajectory are fundamentally connected, and you can use these tools together to craft your shots. This is fairly reliable but can introduce some variability you may not love, especially in windy conditions.

There are also setup changes that will affect the trajectory of your shots. Where you place your ball (or stand relative to the ball) in your setup will affect how high your shots come out. Imagine a line parallel to your target line. The farther forward along that line you place the ball in your setup, the higher you will hit the ball. The farther you place it back, the lower. This is because placing the ball forward or back will change how steeply you strike the ball, thereby changing the dynamic loft of your clubs. This is a good tool around the margins. Know, however, that if you change your setup dramatically, you will introduce all kinds of variability and potential mishits into your game. It's a lot easier to change the actual loft by changing clubs than changing the dynamic loft by moving the ball around. That said, you should know this is a tool at your disposal.

---

54 Note that some golfers will tell you that there's no such thing as a straight shot, that all balls have some left or right spin. However slight, every shot should be played to have some of that spin. Again, no matter how slight. I think this is bullshit. There are straight shots, and you can learn to hit them. They just happen to be a lot harder to hit. My technique is basically the one I described above for my stock three wood or dinky drive: hold the body very firm, clench your abs, and commit fully to the shot. This, coincidentally, is the absolute best shot to hit into the wind. In good conditions, it loses 15% power off my stock shot, but nothing penetrates the breeze better.

Finally, there are swing changes you can make that will promote high or low ball flights. For me, a longer swing with looser-feeling arms will really jack the ball way up in the air, and a shorter, more controlled swing will keep the ball down.

Your final tool in this space is just a straight feel. That is a real thing, but it will take lots of trial and error for you to get it right, so proceed with caution here. Attempting to modify your full shots through feel is something advanced golfers do all the time. Nonetheless, many golfers would benefit from taking it out of their game. Your scoring shots are the few stock shots that you're most comfortable with. In adverse conditions, look first to stay in your comfort zone and change your shots with clubs rather than with your swing. I know that I've said it a million times, but the swing you're most comfortable with is the swing that will hold up under pressure.

Those are the primary tools for affecting trajectory. In my view, changing clubs is the most effective tool and least likely to introduce error into your swings. After that is setup, swing change, and spin. Great golfers will use all of these in concert to choose shots, but mostly will play their stock shots. The best way to control trajectory overall is to keep each aspect within a tight range rather than attempting to make extreme changes to any one of these elements. Practice each element, and you'll be one step closer to controlling your ball in the air.

SWING AWAY

So that's everything I think about full golf shots, how to learn to hit them, and how to think about hitting them. It is by no means a comprehensive study of publicly available golf knowledge, but it will help more or less anyone improve. I tried, where something was just my opinion, or my feel, to say that. This is so you won't take anything I've made up to serve my golf swing as canon. I admit I am fallible.

Really, though, the best approach to learning to swing is not to take anything as canon, even if Tiger Woods and Harvey Penick said it. When Nas said, "Born alone, die alone, no crew to keep my crown or throne," he probably wasn't thinking about the golf swing, but his wisdom still applies. Your swing is 100% your own. It resides in your nervous system, brain, and body. You have to learn it yourself through practice and repetition. Nothing anyone can say in print, video, or to your damn face can change that.

I hope that after reading my thoughts on the golf swing, novice and intermediate golfers can use this as a framework to guide their own exploration and practice. I also hope that advanced golfers, even those better than me, will still be able to take my thoughts and maybe reconsider how they did something in a swing, some approach or swing thought, and get better from refining their process there. Either way, now you know how I think ball-striking works.

CHAPTER 4

CLUBS

So far, this book has been agnostic to what club you're swinging. This is because, from a broad perspective, the principles of setup, backswing, tempo, and strike are largely the same with every club and shot type. At a certain point, though, this generalization breaks down and can no longer be true. Each club requires a slightly different approach; knowing these differences will help you better think your way around the course.

If you've seen the classic Kevin Costner film *Tin Cup*, you know that a great player can use just one club for a whole round. Utilizing different shots, shaping the ball around obstacles, and hitting stingers, piss missiles, and/or hellacious seeds is really fun. The truth is, though, this style of play rarely makes for good golf among the proletariat. You carry fourteen clubs for a reason, and you hit them all a little bit differently. As I've echoed throughout this book, I don't think there's one right way to hit a golf ball, and the same is true for the strike patterns on different clubs. I'll walk you through what I do on a club-by-club basis. You can use this as a baseline, but you should develop your preferences through practice.

HIGH-LOFTED WEDGES. I carry a 58-degree and a 54-degree wedge. I'll talk a bit more about choosing equipment later in this book, but consider your "high-lofted wedges" to include, roughly, your lob wedge and sand wedge. These clubs are primarily designed for very short shots and are often optimized for hitting shots around the greens and out of the sand. When I was young, I marveled at how high I could blast my lob wedge in the air, taking full swings from any lie. The problem with these shots is that when so much energy is translated into shooting the ball in the air, less is translated into the direction of the ball. This can make judging the full swing distance and direction difficult for these clubs. A full swing with my 58-degree wedge might go 75 yards or might go 115, with the same swing speed, just from small variations in the strike of the ball. More than just this, the high floaty ball flight this promotes is extremely susceptible to even light breezes, further spreading out the dispersion. These are scoring clubs. You should be able to drop the ball in a 10-foot circle consistently from 70 yards. That means that this unpredictable floaty ball flight is untenable.

The answer is never hitting high-lofted wedges with more than a three-quarter swing. Sure, there are certain situations when you have to hit the ball over a high obstacle directly in front of you. You need a full-swing flop, but in my experience, this is only four or five times a year. The rest of the time, you should knock the ball down with these clubs to keep it under control.

I make this swing with particularly stable feet and try to keep my torso steady while my arms rotate around me. You have plenty of power to get the ball to the target, so the focus should be on consistency, consistency, consistency. My goal in practicing this shot is to hit the same shot every time. In addition to shortening the swing, I try to promote a downward strike on the ball to compress it against the turf and ensure that it spins when it hits the green. This shot is extremely easy on your body to practice and probably the easiest shot in the game. Every time you're on the range, you should drill it in, leaving you confident when you get near the green to hammer in the dagger on the course.

LOW-LOFTED WEDGES, NINE IRONS, AND EIGHT IRONS. Your shortest clubs are sometimes called scoring clubs. The reality is most of the shots you're hitting with these clubs can't be expected to fall in the 10-foot circle I described above. That said, you should be consistently hitting greens with these, and good players should try to narrow that down even further. I am trying to get these in a quadrant of the green, at least! More often than not, I'm taking dead aim at the pin with my long wedges and short irons.

For reasons similar to your high-lofted wedges, I don't think you should take full swings with these clubs most of the time. First of all, you *never* need to hit these clubs farther. If you think you need a full swing to hit one of these clubs the distance you want, just reach in your bag and grab a longer club. Problem solved. There's no shame in hitting a longer club a shorter distance, and to the extent it gives you more control over the ball, it will make you a better golfer. Plus, you've been doing your Larry Bird drills, so you know exactly how to hit a three-quarter shot right on line.

These clubs tend to be susceptible to the same high, weak ball flight as your high-lofted wedges and should be approached somewhat similarly. That said, I try to make slightly more sweeping contact with these rather than the biting downstroke of my high-lofted wedges. This is because I'm less worried about these clubs getting floaty. And a gentler descent will make you less vulnerable to imperfect turf conditions. Swinging steeply down on a ball after a rainstorm can result in a face full of mud.

Practice these shots nearly as much as your lob and sand wedges, hitting different distances to build a feel. Practice hitting your eight iron 130 yards and your pitching wedge 155 to get a feel for the different strikes you can put on these clubs, then dial in your stock distances for a nice three-quarter swing and rely on that for almost all your shots out on the course. Any variable you can remove from your conscious mind while you're swinging will improve your consistency and make the game easier to play.

SEVEN IRONS. If you haven't seen *Tin Cup*, pay Amazon your three dollars and watch it. You may not see many competent golf swings in the movie, but it nails the ethos of the true golfer. In *Tin Cup*, Kevin Costner fights with his caddy Cheech Marin and then breaks every club in his bag but his seven iron. The seven iron is the platonic ideal golf club. Everything written about golf that doesn't explicitly specify that it concerns another club is written with a seven iron in mind. Your seven iron is the shortest club with which you should be taking full swings, that is, getting that shaft somewhere close to parallel to the ground. While you may still want to use three-quarter swings with your seven iron, you're permitted to rip stick here occasionally, and that's a beautiful thing. Just make sure not to overindex this advice. Even with your seven iron, the smart money is on a slightly less than 100% swing. It just gives you more control.

With this club, I do try to target quadrants of the green or at least halves. You have to accept a reasonable margin of error from 180 yards out. Build this error into your shot choice with the seven iron and longer, and work to avoid trouble around the greens. It's much better to be putting than chipping.

SIX IRON. Six iron is a strong seven iron.

FIVE IRON THROUGH THREE IRON. These are your long irons. Arguably, five iron is a strong six iron. But given loft creep in modern equipment, good players frequently carry their five iron over 200 yards these days. That, my friend, is a long iron, and you should swing accordingly.

These long irons are probably the hardest to hit for most nonelite golfers. A relatively high swing speed is required to get long irons up into the air. For that reason, many players replace them with hybrids, which I discuss below. I find that a nice full swing to help get the ball flying is usually right for these clubs. If I try a three-quarter swing with a four iron, I often struggle to get the clubhead back on the ball soundly and produce mishits or weak little queefs.

I think anxiety is part of the reason these clubs create such a problem for people. We have all seen a full-swing three iron sailing into the trees and taking the player out of the hole. This trauma builds up scar tissue, and many of us are afraid to commit to a shot. This leads us to fail to swing through the ball confidently. The reality is that with a long iron, you need both high swing speeds and center strikes to get the ball up in the air and moving on a piercing trajectory. Without both physical ability and confidence, it's hard to do that. That's why God made hybrids.

I like to emphasize a sweeping motion on contact with these clubs. It's still a slightly downward strike, but the most level of your irons. You don't have to work to get the ball up in the air; just swing free, hit it solid on a line toward your target, and watch the ball fly away. When hitting a long iron, I aim at the dead center of the green. Some pros might be able to choose halves or quadrants to aim at, but when I'm 220 yards away, hitting the green at all is an accomplishment. Aiming to the dead center gives you the most room for error. The exception is if there's bad trouble to one side of the green but not the other, then I will err away from the trouble. Being in the greenside rough is much better than being in a gorge or water hazard. Bear this in mind and be thoughtful in picking your aim with these clubs. Even a perfect strike from this distance has a relatively large error margin.

TWO IRON OR DRIVING IRON. These clubs have come into popularity recently as swing speeds have increased, and some players have grown dissatisfied with five woods or hybrids. Modern players mostly use these clubs off the tee to produce penetrating ball flights with relative accuracy. I carry a two iron, which I love dearly. My club is a pure two, without any of the extra weightings that come with a modern driving iron. For me, it's a perfect club. I carry it 230 yards, it penetrates any wind, I can work it either way, and I am totally confident hitting it. For you, though, a different club might be better. The best way to choose among these clubs is to feel them out. I love the precision of the two iron. Some people love the forgiveness of driving irons.

Because they tend to be so useful off the tee, you may use these long irons many times a round and find them to be high-value clubs.[55] Because they're so frequently hit off the tee, I like an almost upward swing at the time of contact. For me, it's the closest to a driver swing. Even a three wood, with its large head and high loft, will get the ball up in the air more easily than a driving iron.

I mentioned that I carry a stock two iron. Part of the reason is that it's a little bit easier to hit off the turf, which I frequently do. For this shot, consider it basically the same as your three or four iron. You will just need a little bit more swing speed to control it. If you

---

[55] Remember, even here, the goal is not to hit the ball as far as you can. Instead, it is to gap your clubs tightly and consistently so that you have a club for every distance you will need in a round. When I watch some of the really long hitters out there, like Kyle Berkshire, I am constantly blown away by how boneheaded their gapping is. Kyle will hit his five iron 280 yards. This makes no goddamn sense. Money shots are always going to come within 80 yards of the hole and require a high-lofted wedge. So if you're stretching your long irons out this far and are still only permitted fourteen clubs in your back, you necessarily have more yardage between clubs. To me, these wide gaps produce no obvious benefit and introduce all kinds of uncertainty in club choice. If the distance between your stock clubs is only 10 to 15 yards max, you will almost always have a stock swing to the green. If you're Kyle Berkshire and it's 30 yards between clubs, you're going to find yourself doing mental gymnastics to figure out what shot to hit. In my opinion, that won't stand up to pressure.

have that, I say go for it. I love this club. If you don't, maybe consider a hybrid.

ONE IRON. Lee Trevino said that if you ever get caught in a thunderstorm, hold up your one iron. Even God can't hit a one iron.

HYBRIDS. Hybrids add mass behind the clubface to make longer clubs easier to hit. This is achieved by moving the center of the mass lower and farther back from the face to reduce the moment of inertia or something like that. I'm a lawyer, not an engineer, and I can't really explain that to you. That said, it works. Hybrids hit the ball higher and farther in the air with the same swing speed. That's why these clubs are a great choice for golfers with slightly slower swing speeds. Practically, too, they're just really easy to hit from any lie. You pretty much just have to nick the ball with the face to hit a long shot with a hybrid.

For golfers with higher swing speeds, hybrids might not be ideal. Hit hard, hybrids tend to launch the ball too high in the air and lead to floaty shots that are susceptible to wind. When I played hybrids, I liked a pretty neutral but somewhat downward strike, similar to a six or five iron. I've never found these clubs particularly accurate, so I recommend aiming at dead center on the green. In reality, amateur players who aim dead center outperform those aiming for the pin in general, so you'll likely find this strategy beneficial in even more situations than I specifically recommend here.

FIVE WOODS AND THREE WOODS. The only person I know to carry a five wood is Tiger. I don't know what they're good for or their advantages or disadvantages over a hybrid. If you have one and you like it, more power to you, but I can't give you much advice here.

LET THE BIG DOG EAT

Three woods, on the other hand, are magical clubs, and I've studied them closely. Because of the visual similarity and because they're the two longest clubs in your bag, you would be forgiven for thinking that a three wood is similar to a driver. Something like a short driver or a light driver. The reality is a three wood isn't like a driver at all. On tour, players change drivers every year or two to advertise for their sponsors' next big thing and keep up with changes in technology. Three woods, on the other hand, will stay in bags for five, ten, or fifteen years. While drivers are made primarily to hit the ball as far and accurately off the tee as possible, distance doesn't matter with three woods. The key is that it hits the ball farther than your two iron and not as far as your driver. That's all.

The defining characteristic of a good three wood is versatility and consistency. When I can't hit driver off the tee because of a hazard, I want to be able to hit three wood to get as close to the hole as possible while keeping the trouble out of play. When I'm in the fairway 280 yards from the green, I want to be able to hit three wood. Even out of weird lies or the rough, I like to be able to trust this club to put a line on the ball and send it pretty deep without making any huge misses that will take me out of a hole or round. For this reason, my three-wood swing is more compact and directed than my driver swing (which I describe below) or my two-iron swing. The three wood itself will do all the work of getting the ball in the air and hitting it far, so the main purpose of my swing here is to make sure it gets on line consistently. This is the club you use when you have to be accurate, so you must make it a priority to be accurate with it.[56]

With the three wood, I like to swing somewhere between a full swing and three-quarters, never under any circumstance past parallel, and tense my abdominal wall throughout the swing to keep myself steady. On the strike, I like a slightly downward strike to keep the dynamic loft of the club low and prevent my ball from getting too spinny or floaty in the air. Because this club is so personal to its users, you might want to develop different swing quirks, but remember, accuracy and consistency are fundamental here. Figure out a plan that works for you and keep yourself comfortable whenever you swing it.

DRIVER. The big dog itself. Tee it high and let it fly, my children. Dougie is going deep.

The purpose of your driver is to move the ball as close to the hole as possible without getting you into too much trouble along the way. Almost all the time, with driver in hand, you want to crank up a nice full swing and take a big whack at the ball. This is the point of the driver, first of all, and second of all, I have always found it harder to hit a driver on line with anything less than a full, hard swing. As mentioned several times in this book, a driver is best hit on a slight upswing. To accomplish this, most players will move the ball slightly toward the front foot, the left foot for a right-handed player, to allow

---

56 I've met a lot of people who told me they couldn't hit their three wood well. To this I say, practice cures all. Make accuracy a point of emphasis in your training, and over time you will improve. Don't complain about not getting the reward for the work you didn't do.

LET THE BIG DOG EAT

the swing to finish at the bottom and just tick upward to the ball for contact. I go past parallel on this swing and focus on making a nice full-shoulder turn. There is an impulse to jump at the ball, but power comes from your turn and your legs, so focus on your backswing and sequencing, and you'll be getting the most out of your shots.

Hitting the ball far is most of the point of a driver. It's much easier to put your ball in birdie range from 50 yards than 80 yards, from 80 than 100, and so on.[57] A whole subgroup of tour pros play "bomb and gouge" golf, where they hit the ball well over 300 yards and don't worry whether they're in the rough or fairway because the flip wedges they're hitting in will always be easier than Brian Harman's seven iron from 170 back. If you can hit the ball this far, this is a sound strategy worth considering. It's always important to keep yourself out of trouble, though. The rough is not the same as trouble (except at certain US Open courses like Bethpage Black, where they grow the rough so long and thick that you can hardly get a nine iron out of there). For every tee shot, you should know where the trouble is and make sure to avoid it. This is discussed in the strat-

---

[57] Note: some players prefer to hit the ball to the distance of one of their stock shots. They can take a nice full swing and hit a 70-yard shot into the green rather than have to hit a dinky 40-yarder. I kind of think this has to be wrong. Closer shots, I would guess, are easier on average, even if they *feel* less comfortable. That said, there are some compelling advantages of being slightly farther away. For instance, when playing onto firm greens, a full swing will produce a higher trajectory and more backspin, both of which will help keep the ball on the putting surface. Honestly, this kind of calculus comes into play only rarely, once every two or three rounds at most, and you should probably do what you are comfortable with. Remember that you have to practice and consider the shots you're leaving yourself to know what you're comfortable with. Like Big Sean said, it's grind day from Friday to next Friday.

Clubs

egy section below. But with a driver in my hands, I will make sure to physically aim my body fully away from the trouble. Drivers are not precise clubs. I have seen many amateurs aim over toward the shit, try to execute a difficult shot, and then beat themselves up when they fuck up and hit it in. Even great players are not that accurate with the big dog: aim away from the shit and give yourself as much room for error as possible.

Also important with the driver is knowing your spin. Almost all drives will have either cut spin or draw spin on them, which over 300 yards will make a big difference in where the ball ends up. You should be able to either control the direction of that spin or else know the kind of spin you impart on the ball and aim accordingly. You have to play for your spin. If you hit persistent cuts, don't aim for the center of the fairway and hope you can control your ball this time. Aim left (for a right-handed golfer), and make sure you take that bad miss out.

There's one final special swing with the driver that you need to learn. Like the tight, controlled three-wood swing I hit when trying to hit the green, I like to practice a compact driver swing. I don't take the club back as far. I tense my abs and feel myself in control and balanced over the ball. I find that learning this swing helps me be significantly more accurate off the tee, albeit at the expense of 40–50 yards. When trying to hit greens or other very narrow targets, and driver is your only choice, having this swing in your back pocket is worth it. I'm still swinging HARD, though. Don't forget that.

CHAPTER 5

CHIPPING

A GOLFER ACHIEVES A "GREEN IN REGULATION" WHEN THEY REACH the green in one stroke on a par 3, two strokes on a par 4, or three strokes on a par 5.[58] The previous sections have attempted to teach you the physical skills to reach the green in regulation. And the forthcoming strategy section gives you the knowledge to implement those skills.

Even with all my knowledge inside you, you should know that you still won't always be able to reach the green in regulation. Even the best golfers in the world miss greens frequently, and you will too. This is the realm of chipping.

To make par after missing a green in regulation is called "getting up and down." Getting up and down is one of the core skills of great golfers. Sometimes this is known as "scrambling." In this chapter I

---

58 The few courses with par 6 holes can fuck right off.

walk you through strategies and techniques to chip effectively and get up and down as often as possible. I give a fulsome description below, but I want to start with three simple points that, on their own, should make anyone who follows them a halfway decent scrambler.

FIRST. Your hands must be in front of the ball at contact to chip well. This means your contact on chips should come at a descending angle, as in most of your full swings.

Many amateurs fear chips. They worry that they won't be able to get the ball in the air, and so they compensate by trying to hit up on the ball as if to somehow pull it up in the air. To do this, they hold their hands back, letting the clubhead pass their hands and start to move up. Thus, at contact, the club is already ascending. This is skull city, brother. This common technique leads amateurs to contact the ball low on the face or against the leading edge, leaving it briskly skipping across the green and, in all likelihood, setting the golfer up for the same shot, or worse, again. So don't do that! Hit down on the ball.

The wedges that most of us use around the green have a lot of lofts to make it easy to get up in the air without much clubhead speed. In other words, they do the work for you. This gives the golfer the freedom to hit down on the ball, creating the best opportunity for good contact, and still hit delicate chip shots that don't roll too far out on the green. The best way to ensure that you're hitting at this optimal angle is to have your hands ahead of the ball at contact, guaranteeing a downward strike. Since the club is traveling downward, it will compress the ball against the turf a little bit, which will also impart some backspin. This backspin helps chips land soft and stick on the green. This point alone will go a long way to taking out most of the really bad shots around the green.

SECOND. The next cue, as important as leading with the hands, not the clubhead, is to continue through the ball. I discussed this in the chapter on the full swing, and it's equally important to chipping. Around the greens, many players, in an attempt to control the distance of the ball, chop at the ball and decelerate. This error creates the dreaded chunk, where the ball goes next to nowhere. After you hit these, you might hear your playing partners groan to themselves. Other errors, too, emanate from this fundamental mistake because it undermines your confidence.

You have to accelerate through the chip. I'll admit that some downhill shots are so delicate that it's almost impossible to adhere to this tenet, but 95% of the time, an easy move through the ball will serve you well.

You should practice acceleration so that it becomes second nature. Take short backswings, and then accelerate down and through the shot. If you have to hit it 10 feet, the backswing will be very short! But that's okay because your overall control and consistency will be at their highest when you're hitting through the ball. It's tough to make delicate chips this way at times, but if you commit to the technique, you'll learn to do it with finesse, and it will serve you well for the rest of your days.

THIRD. Get the ball on the green. This is seemingly obvious. You're trying to get the ball in the hole, 20 feet away, and aiming dead at the green. Of course, you're trying to get the ball on the green. But I've seen tons of people miss the green on chips; I've done it myself! But we never, ever, should.

I think the insight here pertains less to any technique than it is strategic. In order of priority, it's far more important that you get the ball on the green, anywhere on the green, than that you get it very close to the hole. Hitting the ball into the center of the green and having two putts is not ideal, but duffing a chip or skulling it over the green because you were trying to do something too difficult or touchy is a disaster. In that case, you have used a stroke but have not improved your position. You will be left with the same shot again or worse, and your confidence will be shot. That is how triple bogeys are made around the green.

It took me years to understand this, so I hope to help you short-circuit that process. When you're short-sided, have water past the green, are on bad turf, or are otherwise facing a very difficult chip with a large potential for error, take the easy way out! You can consider going straight at the cup, but sometimes it's totally correct to just aim for center of the green and live to fight another day. You can't always be aggressive.

As a younger man, I attempted to get the ball as close as possible to the hole 100% of the time. I paid the price many times with this strategy. Taking a safer shot when it's called for will lower your golf scores and make you a better golfer. This is not to say you should never attempt a difficult chip, but you have to respect risk. When making this decision, remember that getting the ball on the green is priority number one, and any shot that may compromise that priority should be handicapped accordingly. Apply this thinking, and I guarantee you will take several double and triple bogeys out of your game. These add up.

HOW TO CHIP

With those three points in mind, here's a more specific breakdown of how chipping works.

The chip is a short stroke taken from around the green with the goal of getting your ball as close to the hole as possible. Most of the time, the golfer's goal when chipping is to get up and down, hitting the chip relatively close to the hole and making the remaining putt. Occasionally, players will try to make chips outright. Different kinds of chip shots are situationally appropriate at different times. And the techniques that golfers use to make chips are different from those to get up and down, so it's important to consider what you're trying to do with a specific chip shot and visualize the shot you plan to hit.

In assessing a chip shot, first, consider your location and condition. Are you on firm turf? Is the ground a little wet? Are you above the hole or below it? How much green is between you and the hole? Are there any obstacles between you and the ball that you have to clear to get the ball onto the green or to the hole? All these factors should be weighed in considering what type of shot you want to hit (different kinds of chip shots are discussed below).

Once this shot is chosen, you must choose a club to hit that shot. Historically, most players have carried at least a pitching and a sand wedge. These days, most people carry a high-lofted lob wedge as well. I carry four wedges: a 46-degree, a 50-degree, a 54-degree, and a 58-degree. Any of these clubs could be appropriate for chipping. Your choice will depend partly on the club's properties and personal preference.

In general, lower-lofted clubs like nine irons are effective for shots that run out after hitting the green. Higher-lofted wedges like a 56- or 58-degree will land softer and stop sooner after hitting the green. But you could probably hit a 54-degree sand wedge and a nine iron at a similar trajectory if you really wanted to![59] That is where personal preference comes in.

There is no one right club, though. Many players always chip with the same club and perform extremely well. Some people assess and use a different club all the time. Hell, some people chip with a three wood. Comfort is very important to chipping, so experiment and see what feels right to you. If you're a novice, start with your highest-lofted wedge and work backward.

Now, knowing the shot you plan to hit and having a club in hand, you can set up to the ball. I prefer to address the ball with some slight forward shaft lean to promote the forward hands and downward strike I emphasized above.

---

59 One note worth considering. In my view, the difference in club choice can be greater than trajectory alone would suggest. I used to try to hit my 58-degree wedge low when I wanted it to run up a slope, only to find it checking up and slowing down dismayingly often. I believe that a higher-lofted club will stop sooner, even when it's hit low, than will a lower-lofted club. Generally, this means that I use my highest-lofted wedge when hitting downhill or on flat ground and choose a lower-lofted club when hitting uphill.

　　　　　　　　　　　　　LET THE BIG DOG EAT

Depending on the shot you want to hit and the club in your hand, you may want to either open or close the clubface to add or take loft off the club you chose. This is done by rotating the club in your hands, which will either open it and add loft, or close it and take loft off.

Note that putting the clubhead back to address with a neutral stance and a closed or open face will not produce a viable setup. You always want the club flat behind the ball at address and aimed down the target line. To accommodate this, you have to move your body's alignment off the target line until the club is on line, opening your body for loft added and closing it for loft taken off (note that chipping with a very closed body is ill-advised, so you may want to simply club up in this situation).

Beyond alignment, you want a similar athletic stance as in full swing, though I like to allow my arms to hang a little softer, which helps with touch. Grip the club just firmly enough to keep it in place, take it back, and strike through the ball.

It is surprisingly difficult to make a good strike on such a short shot. To do so, you'll be well served by keeping your hands ahead of the ball and striking through it, as I suggested above. That's assuming you get there, make good contact, and choose your shot well. Most of the success of your shot here will be in how hard you strike the ball. This is "touch."

Some of your shots may miss slightly off line, but if you practice enough, you should be able to dial these misses in considerably. Just line up square to your target line and practice getting the ball out on line consistently for a few hours, and you should find control pretty easy to learn. This is not a long swing; don't overthink it.

Touch, on the other hand, is not easily learned. All players continue to refine this skill throughout their lives. I think, for the most part, touch is learned only through repeated practice. That said, learning to hit different shots and think strategically can go a long way to taking the importance of extreme finesse out of your game. If you only know how to play high chip shots, getting close to a hole on a slope above you will take a lot of touch, but if you learn to run the ball with your irons, it will be much easier. Sometimes it's a good idea to work smarter rather than, or in addition to, harder.

Touch is particularly responsive to practice frequency. After taking time away from the game, I have observed that chipping is the first thing to go. On the other hand, the thing that benefits the most from playing regularly is this touch around the greens. If you can find the time to hit chips every day, you will undoubtedly find that your touch improves. When I was a kid, I remember my dad going to the golf course to chip every day in the summer. This practice paid dividends for him, and it will for you too.

While I think the best chipping practice is simply frequent practice rooted in the three principles I described above, there are a few chipping drills I find myself going back to again and again.

I like to practice by focusing on my chip's landing spot rather than just trying to get it as close to the hole as possible. I will take a shag bag (a tool that carries a hundred balls or so and makes it easy to pick them all up) out to the range and drill chips for a couple of hours at a time. When I'm emphasizing this kind of training, I set up three or so zones to chip into and cycle through them. This drill helps to force you to consider each shot. I believe that work rooted in conscious effort rather than mindless repetition is especially effective. Remember that if you just go through the motions, you will risk reinforcing your bad habits and thus making it even harder to improve.

Another way I try to drill in chipping is to use only three or four balls and take my putter out onto the practice green to make the putts after I hit the chips. This obviously slows down the practice, but it emphasizes scoring, which, after all, is the entire goal of chipping and playing competitive golf. Plus, I think it might help people who are nervous over short putts.

Chipping is pretty simple. Set up well, strike down and through the ball, plan your shots wisely, and practice as much as possible. If you do all this, you'll do fine.

CHIP SHOTS

With a general technique and strategy for chipping in hand, you can consider some advanced techniques. Many strong wedge players do hit the same basic shot every time, but if you can learn a few other shots well, you may create some up-and-down opportunities. Variety in turf condition, speed of green, and location of the ball and the pin will all occasionally demand different shots.

Most golfers have a stock chip shot that they prefer to hit on relatively flat, even turf conditions around a flat green. I use my

58-degree wedge, line up dead square to my target line, and just try to bump the ball on my line. This pretty, high chip doesn't roll out too much on the green. Other players prefer different shots! For example, I have observed that many players from the UK or Texas have an easier time running the ball with a nine iron. I believe that this is because they're more familiar with very firm turf conditions that call for this kind of shot.

Once your stock shot is dialed, all other chip shots will be a variation on that standard. I grew up playing in slightly damp turf conditions that benefit from a steep, extremely clean strike of the ball. When I play in firmer conditions, I modify my stock shot by taking more club, which might be a 50-degree wedge, and bumping the ball to let it roll out farther.

This shot is sometimes called the "bump and run." The goal of the bump and run is to hit the ball just on the green and get it rolling like a putt. It's good to use in firm turf conditions because "tight" lies, that is, firm lies without much grass, can be less forgiving of poor strikes, and firm greens will tend to roll even when you hit the ball high. The low bump swing is more forgiving and removes some of this variability.[60]

Bump and runs can be hit with any club you like. My club choice is informed by the degree of uphill or downhill slope to my shot.

---

[60] I have a theory as to why this is. I think that it takes more total energy to hit a high chip than a low chip. A lot of that energy is converted into height on good shots, but on mishits, all that energy is converted directly into a horizontal vector. This difference in the force vector between good strikes and bad strikes creates inconsistency. Because intentionally low shots will be low whether hit well or mishit, they're more forgiving. Just a theory.

As I mentioned above, shots hit with lower lofted clubs release much farther out on the green. When chipping uphill, the release on a shot will be sharply curtailed. For this reason, I use nine irons, eight irons, or even seven irons when chipping up steep slopes, and if the slope is steep enough, you may need even more. Nothing is worse than trying to chip up a slope, not getting it there, and seeing the ball roll back down to you, so make sure you take enough club! Whether hitting a 50-degree wedge or a five iron, the swing to bump the ball is roughly the same, a nice smooth backswing, and then low and sweeping through the ball. You should see the ball pop up a few inches onto the green and then release to the hole.

Sometimes, when the turf conditions are very firm, or the ball doesn't have to roll over much fringe, the best chip shot isn't a chip at all. Pull out the old Texas wedge, a.k.a. your putter, in these situations.

Putting from off the green can be a tricky thing and requires its own practice. I have never been particularly good at it and find it hard to judge. That said, there is received wisdom that you will always be more precise with a putter than a wedge. I have seen many people use these shots very effectively. I think this technique merits experimentation and effort. The exact conditions that call for a putt from off the green will depend on your comfort and skill level. But for me, any time I'm very close to the green or going over very flat turf, I will consider it. I once saw someone try to putt out of a bunker. That was fucking stupid. Don't do that.

Hitting the ball downhill on the green usually requires a different strategy. Low running shots may end up picking up speed and roll off the other side. So shots must be hit higher and softer (or placed extremely carefully) to keep them on the green (and get them close to the hole). For these shots, I like to open the clubface and hit some variation of a flop shot. Note that a true flop shot, the kind that Phil Mickelson sometimes breaks out using his 64-degree wedge, is extremely difficult to hit and should be used only in extreme circumstances. That said, the principles of the shot, used judiciously, will allow you to hit soft shots that end up closer to the hole.

You want to open up the clubface and your body for flop-type shots. When the club is open, loft is added so that your 58-degree wedge acts more like a 70-degree wedge and can get the ball up faster. I like to take a relatively long swing for high shots and feel like the club is coming up and away from my body. This is because my body is no longer facing the target line. So by letting my arms come away, the club can move on a relatively straight path back from the ball and return square to the target line while still being open, thus maintaining the added loft. Swing through the ball and let it pop up in the air, making sure not to let your wrists release through impact.

One swing thought that has been especially useful to me in hitting these shots is to think about my weight transition. Keeping your weight over your lead foot through your flop swings will help you get down and through the ball at impact. This produces clean buttery flops that land softly. Many players will fall onto their back foot at some point in their flop swing in an attempt to hoist the ball up into the air, but this will only create sad skulled shots and incon-sistency.

Flop shots have a high risk and fall into two main buckets. First, when the ball sits in a fluffy lie, for instance, sitting up in rough, there's a real risk that your club might pass under the ball and not move it at all or move it only slightly. If you see that you have a lie like this, take some flop off the shot by closing the clubface and your body (relative to the already open stance you would have used) and trust that the fluffy lie will contribute to a higher and softer shot on its own. The second risk, which is more common, is that you will skull the ball.

The key to avoiding this is to work on your first principles of chipping. Even now, you must keep your hands in front of the ball and hit through it. Unlike in a full swing, where pulling up is rarely the problem in a player's swing, people tend to pull up on chips because they aren't hitting through the ball. I also like to feel the club almost thumping the turf as I'm hitting. When I keep the club low at impact, this swing feel helps me ensure that I don't skull it and the ball comes out soft.[61]

You will have to feel out your own game to learn how to gently place a flop shot, but I generally try to land the ball at almost a dead

---

61 The amount of bounce on your wedge will affect the way you play these shots. Clubs with very low bounce tend to dig into the turf but are easy to get under the ball and so are favored by highly skilled players who like extreme flops. If you have higher bounce, you may not be able to slide the club under the ball as easily, but you can feel the bounce interact with the turf and deliver the club to the ball softly. Try out different bounces and get to know your own clubs to get a feel for how this will interact with turf conditions to create predictable shots for your game.

stop, and then roll with just the slope of the green down toward the hole. This skill, hitting a ball up in the air and having it land in a specific spot on the green, is much more difficult to master than bumping it and rolling like a chip. For this reason, you should choose your stock chip or bump and run when given a choice. The flop is really just for those few situations that truly demand it. I'll talk more about playing percentages later in this book.

The final chip shot I would advocate adding to your game is a spinny shot. This involves striking down sharply on the ball so that it squirts out farther onto the green than a bump and run. The ball should then spin dramatically, take one hop on the green, and stop or "check up." To play this shot, you will need to understand turf conditions (you can really only spin the ball off the clean fairway or fringe lies), the green conditions (balls will spin more dramatically on softer and slower greens), and the slope (spin will take much more off the ball going uphill, even slightly uphill, than downhill). However, once you get a feel for it, it can be one of the easiest ways to get the ball close to the hole. In wet conditions, it is also doubly effective. First, since you're hitting sharply down on the ball, there is little space to get caught in the soft wet turf and chunk the ball, eliminating some risk. Second, wet greens are far more receptive to spin, and you can stop the ball on a dime. I spin the ball in wet conditions to give myself 2-foot par putts seven days a week, son.

SAND SHOTS

Knowing how to hit all these chips, you also have the tools in your arsenal to hit effective sand shots. Many amateurs fear the sand, and it is intimidating when the lip is high and the sand conditions poor. Most of the time, though, playing typical well-maintained bunkers around the green, the sand is among the easiest chip shots you will have. This is because sand shots (from good sand conditions) are consistent and tend to land softly with a good amount of spin. I promise that if you dedicate time to learning to hit these shots consistently, you'll be able to master them.

If you don't have to get over a difficult lip, take your chips from the sand square. Put the ball slightly forward in your stance, dig your feet into the sand, aim an inch behind the ball, hit down on the sand, and swing through it confidently toward the hole. Done correctly, this should dig the ball out and send it toward the hole, where it will land softly with spin. It's really that simple.

The most common issue players run into with this shot, as with chips in general, is not hitting through the ball. Because you're hitting through the sand, you have to swing harder than you would normally, which is scary and shakes some golfers' confidence. When this happens, they may fail to commit, decelerate through the sand, and chunk the ball. Or they may not take enough sand, afraid of that same deceleration, and send the ball out too hot. These are real issues; the way to avoid them is to practice and build confidence. If you haven't practiced and make one of these errors, it's not because the shot is hard. It's because you haven't put in the work.

If you have a lip to deal with, you must get the ball up in the air. While the stock sand shot can do this, sometimes you'll have to implement your flop techniques here too. To get the ball up in the air, you're essentially doing the same thing you did with your stock swing, just with an open clubface. Set up open and back from the ball and aim an inch and a half behind the ball. Hit down on the sand and feel the club thump down and through. This should blast the ball up into the air and forward onto the green. This is the one time I give you permission not to have your hands in front of the ball at contact. That's acceptable for this shot because when the club is wide open and you're making contact far behind the ball, it's not possible for the clubhead to pass your hands by the time it comes in contact with the ball. Like your square chip shots, confidence is everything, and practice will guide your hand.

DIFFICULT CHIPS

There are a few other special situations you may have to deal with when chipping the ball.

One is very wet lies. These tend to promote chunks. In this situation, I find that it's best to accept that much of your touch is gone because the ground will be so unforgiving that you can't risk being delicate. I take my stock shot and deloft it slightly, allowing the ball to come out low and hard and hoping it will spin. If you can get it within a 5-foot circle of the hole, you are giving yourself a good chance to get up and down, and you should be comfortable with that outcome.

Sometimes you will encounter very bald, hardpan lies. Here, too, most players will stick to their stock shot or bump and run when they're below the hole. These lies tend to promote skulls by bouncing your club into the ball. Again, I like to hit down on the ball, though I don't expect it to spin. Just bump it out and let it roll to the cup. If you're experienced, you can get away with being slightly more aggressive here than on wet lies.

If you find yourself in deep rough, it's generally best to play the shot almost like a sand flop, hitting behind the ball and carrying it out. There will, of course, be other strange and varied situations you will find your ball in around the green. To play them well, you'll have to develop your own game and use a little creativity.

That's all there is to it; chipping can be difficult, but it's not *complicated*. Practice often, practice deliberately, and heed my core pieces of advice: keep your hands ahead of the ball at contact, hit down on the ball and through it, and use sound strategy in your risk-taking. If you do this, you'll find yourself developing a stronger chipping game. Getting up and down is a core skill to playing great golf, and a great feeling when you achieve it. Whenever you're around the green, you should believe that you can get the ball up and in the hole. That doesn't mean always playing the most aggressive shot; your first goal must be to get the ball on the green. If you have a 15-foot putt, you have a real chance of making it. If you're in the long grass on the other side of the green because you tried to get too touchy and skulled your downhill chip, not so much.

Most of all, don't beat yourself up. If you can't execute a shot, ask yourself if you have practiced it. If you haven't, then you shouldn't expect to be getting it right. I've seen too many players convince themselves that they're "bad at chipping" because they struggle with difficult shots. Put in the work, and touch will follow. With time, you will figure out how to make the most out of your chip shots to leave yourself the most favorable putts.

CHAPTER 6

PUTTING

DRIVE FOR SHOW, PUTT FOR DOUGH. THAT'S HOW THE SAYING GOES. I told you earlier in this book that if you want to play solid golf, the best place to focus your efforts is on your full swings. You should never forget that without getting to the green, your putting doesn't mean shit.

If you want to play *great* golf, though, putting is everything. I have seen many golfers who strike the ball well give it all up on the greens. I've often heard, "They hit the ball great, can't putt though." And that's the end of the story. If you can't putt, you can't compete in this game.

Putting may not be the first thing you should work on when learning the game. But from the moment you can hit a green in regulation, a huge portion of your focus in practice should be dedicated to putting.[62]

The flat stick is a mysterious mistress; you have to learn its ways and unspool its secrets before it gives you what you desire. Sometimes it will feel like your putter can do no wrong, and the hole will look 10 feet wide. Someday, I guarantee, you will stand 3 feet from the hole and shake while you wonder why it's so hard to get that little ball to drop.

Brilliant putting is an admirable goal. Some players make their whole game on their talent on the greens. If you can find that in you, it will take you to the next level. In my view, though, the key to improving with the putter is not to attempt to be brilliant from the start. In fact, I think the seeming ease of putting is a psychological stumbling block for many players. The fact that it is so simple makes it all the more frustrating when we fail.

To become a great putter, you have to emphasize sustained, focused practice dedicated to making incremental improvements around the margin. Dialing down your misses until most of your three putts become two putts, and more of your 10-footers go in. Over time, practicing in this deliberate, incremental way, an average putter can become a really good one and compete.

---

62 Harvey Penick suggests that you devote 90% of your practice time to the short game, and if you have a solid swing already and want to win, I can't fault him too much. If you're missing greens, though, then that should be your focus. Don't neglect your long game to adhere to some ideal. The areas of your game where you lose the most strokes are the ones that you should give the most attention to.

HOLDING THE PUTTER

Many people I respect have told me that Ben Crenshaw was the greatest putter who ever lived. As best as I can tell, this is attributed to pure talent. In his *Little Red Book*, Harvey Penick, who taught Crenshaw, says that he tried to keep the young Ben off the course so that he wouldn't learn how to do something wrong by accident. There is one universality from Crenshaw's approach, though, that all golfers mention. He held the putter so lightly that it was like a feather in his hand, which he felt gave him the best feel over the putter's head. As far as I know, all great putters have held the putter lightly, and you should too. If you grip the club too tightly, you'll likely make sudden jerking movements with your tensed muscles. The putting stroke is a smooth back-and-forth, one connected motion, and a light grip promotes this.

The putting grip is different from the one you use for your full swing and chips. A traditional putting grip uses an overlap and cradles the club gently in the fingers. There are also many home-grown, half-baked, and sometimes very successful nontraditional grips that you may see at your local municipal track or on the PGA tour. These grips often come paired with idiosyncratic technologies like belly and claw putters. Some people use these to great effect. Which one might be right for you, though, I cannot say, nor will I even go through the multitude of them here. I will tell you my thoughts from my own experiments in the area. You can use that as a baseline for your personal experimentation and development.

I played for a long time with a Ping Zing 2 putter from 1984 with the original pistol grip. The thin hard grip felt great in my hands, and I felt complete control of the head on long putts. This grip gave me a great feel of the ball, or so I thought, but I found myself missing a ton of short putts.

Everyone in the world (except Tiger)[63] misses short putts occasionally. Some people struggle with short putts, while others don't. I think the difference comes from a few innate qualities, particularly central nervous system acuity (hand-eye coordination) and sympathetic nervous system response to stress (nerves). There also might be some increase in that sympathetic nervous system response modulated by past trauma (emotional scar tissue). The reality is that most of those things are difficult to change. However, the effect of those qualities on short putting can be dampened by a putting stroke that emphasizes large muscles over the small twitchy ones in your forearms.

When I started struggling with short putts, I added a fat Super-Stroke grip to my putter. Because your fingers are wider with the SuperStroke, your hands and wrist have less play in the putting motion, which brings more large muscles in and gives deficits in hand-eye coordination or excessive nerves less chance to mess you up on short putts. Changing to this fat grip helped me make far more short putts, and seeing those balls roll in gave me more confidence

---

[63] I heard a story once, and I don't know if it's apocryphal or not, but I heard that Tiger didn't miss a putt inside 5 feet during competition for something like a decade.

LET THE BIG DOG EAT

everywhere on the greens. Now I don't fear the short ones; I can feel this confidence spill over into my other putts. This has helped me play better golf overall. That said, even after doing this for over a year, I still don't think my feel for long putts is as good as it was with the skinny grip. Every change you make in your putting equipment will come with benefits and trade-offs.

This is the full extent of my opinion on putting grips and technology. If you can use a thin grip and rarely yank your short putts, then that's probably good for you. If you struggle with the shorties, though, consider the fatter grip. Jon Rahm uses a skinny little grip and is a phenomenal putter. Jordan Spieth uses a fat grip, and he might be even better. It is most important that your gear fits you. Some players use more eccentric techniques and technologies, like the arm-lock and the claw, to try to increase this effect. These might be effective, but I have never tried them, so I'm unqualified to advise on their use. As with everything else, try them out, find something you feel confident with, and practice it until you can do it well.

MARK AND REPLACE YOUR BALL

In putting, as with your other shots, setup is the first fundamental to consider. Once you're safely on the green (or just off, on the fringe) and you have your putter in hand, the first step to learning to putt is setup. The first element of setup for a putt is the ball. Suppose you're putting from anywhere on the green. In that case, you can mark your ball, pick it up, and place it back in the same spot with any orientation you choose (i.e., you can rotate the ball so that any portion you choose faces up).

First, I should note that you should always do the following: except for 2-foot and shorter putts that you're extremely confident you will make, and which you can, therefore, sometimes play out of turn to "finish up," you should mark your ball every time before you putt.[64] Pick your ball up, clean it, and replace it when you set up to make your putt. This ritual forces you to take some time before hitting the ball and keeps you from rushing your putts. If you're upset about the last shot, it forces you to go through a motion to help you cool your head and regain focus.

It will also help you initiate a standard routine. I think developing this kind of routine is the best way to clear your mind, eliminate nerves, and build a putting stroke that will stand up to pressure. In my routine, I walk my putt, view it from all four sides, place my ball, pick up my mark, choose an intermediate spot along my line and take a practice stroke from there, move back to my putt and take a practice stroke from there, place my club behind the ball, and putt. You can develop your own technique for getting into your putt, but marking the ball is the crucial part of that routine, and you must do it. I have seen many players hastily jack putts wide of the hole

---

64 Note that this is my edict, not an actual rule of golf. But if you see me out there, you had better be following it.

LET THE BIG DOG EAT

because they were angry and didn't mark the ball. Don't be this person.

Golf balls come with all kinds of markings on them—a standard ball should have at least a number, a line, and some writing. Each mark can be used as a visual cue for your putting. You can choose which mark you wish to be in view when you place your ball. If you aren't satisfied with the marks already printed on your balls at the factory, you can additionally mark them with a pen if you so choose.

The specific markings you choose to orient your ball for putts are a matter of personal preference. Almost all golf balls include a line on the side, and many golfers like to use it to line up their putt. Some, like the Callaway triple track balls, even include multiple lines to further refine this process. Players who like to use this technique will line up the ball's marking on their intended start line, then place the line on the top of their putter up to the ball line and try to hit the putt that way. I did this for a long time, and it's really nice to have an external aiming cue to know what direction to hit the ball while your eyes are looking down. Whenever you're lining up a putt, you will face a moment when you have to visualize your line and stop looking at the hole. This top line on the golf ball can arguably help with that. What's more, I always recommend using an alignment cue in practice, so the line on the ball has many merits.

That said, I now fall into a second school of thought with respect to the line, and adopting my current technique may serve you well, too, if you struggle with the line method. I used the line method for a while, and while I liked the idea that I was lining up perfectly every time, I came to think that it wasn't quite working in practice. Even though I had everything aligned, my ball wasn't consistently starting on the target line. Even more galling, when I hit my putts casually without setting up or even with a wedge, I found that I was getting it on a much better line. My intuitive putting was strong, but my top-aligned putting was inconsistent.

I'm not certain why this was, but I came to think that by using the line for alignment, I was overriding my body's natural ability to hit the ball on a line in response to my intuitive understanding of alignment. The line on top of the balls was causing something in that jumble of signals to come out wrong and produce unsteady strokes. Since then, I have begun placing the ball with a plain white part up, with no alignment information. Instead of using the line on the ball to ensure that I'm properly aligned, I follow a strict routine of finding alignment before each putt and trust that I have done it correctly.

This really works for me! I attribute great personal improvement to this change in technique. It has helped me get back to the feeling of hitting the putt I see rather than the putt marked on the top of the ball. That's not to say that either the top-aligned method or my intuitive method will be right for you. Try out both approaches, give them time to feel out how you play, and you will come to develop your own approach. Just don't be afraid to keep developing that approach as you improve.

HOW TO PUTT

Once you've marked your ball and replaced it on the putting surface, you set up. As ever in golf, you should begin from the ground up. Putting setup, as I have mentioned, can vary wildly. As between players, with the driver, iron, or even chipping around the greens, certain elements of a swing really must be consistent. For the putt, though, I kinda don't think this is true. I mean, if you want to get down to it, the clubface has to be pointing in the direction you want to putt, and I still think that you should accelerate through it to hit it well, but otherwise, the world is your oyster. I'll tell you the basic setup I use, and then you can vary it to suit your needs.

First, find your target line (more on reading greens below, if you would like some tips on discerning what this line might be) and set up your feet in alignment with this target line, ball in the center of your stance with your head over the ball when you putt.[65] Place the putter head behind the ball, with the face perpendicular to the target line. Note that the alignment of your feet and body can change slightly. Many players putt with slightly open or closed stances. Conversely, the putter head must be perfectly perpendicular to the target line at address. The ball will always travel perpendicular to the putter head. So this alignment is essential to ensure that the ball comes out on line.

From this position, the putting motion involves taking the putter away from the ball smoothly, then returning it through the golf ball

---

65 Don't you dare wear a glove while putting, you animal.

exactly in the orientation from the address. As I said, the direction of the ball after impact will always be perpendicular to the putter face at contact. Since you lined it up perpendicular to your target line, returning it to that exact position at contact will create a putt on that chosen line.

There are two approaches to drawing the putter head away from the ball. In one, the putter will move on an arc and open slightly during the takeaway. This movement mirrors the natural tendency of the body to swing clubs around itself. It may feel natural to some people, but because this stroke moves the putter head in three rather than two dimensions, it also might introduce variability and make it relatively difficult to return the club accurately to the address position. Because of this, some golfers attempt to take the clubhead straight back from the ball on a line and straight back through the ball, thus removing some margin for error.

While, in theory, this sounds great, I have always found this straight-back straight-through approach slightly unnatural and sometimes difficult to make consistently. For this reason, even though I think it probably introduces a small amount of error, I prefer some arc in my putting stroke. You may be different, so consider which works best for you.

I have been told that different equipment suits the various strokes, particularly with respect to the weighting of putter heads. People talk about face-balanced and toe-hang putters, but I don't understand this mumbo-jumbo. As I said, I putt with a Ping putter from the 1980s. You may find experimentation with your putter head weighting valuable, but I cannot be your guide here. Consult YouTube or, perhaps, a medium.

It's a little-known fact that while the putter is sometimes called the flat stick, it's not actually flat. Putters have something like half a degree of loft. The reason for this loft is to actually lift the putt slightly at contact with the ball. This helps the ball avoid getting caught up in the grass as it begins moving, thereby getting off line. If you hit down on the ball, however, the dynamic loft will be negative. Your putts will be more likely to get caught up in the turf and start off line, particularly on bumpy greens. For this reason, the ideal contact should be perfectly level, or if there is an error to be made, slightly up on the ball. If you find that this is a problem for you, just move the ball slightly forward in your stance, which will place it farther along in the arc of your putting stroke, on the upswing.

PUTTING WEIGHT

Since you now have dialed in the direction of your putts and the angle of attack of your strike on the ball, the final element of hitting good putts is the weight. "Weight" or touch is the amount of force you put into your putts. In putting, touch really is everything. Even reading the greens poorly, a golfer with correct weight on every putt will rarely three-putt. In so doing, they generally are able to keep themself in competition. Putting with bad touch, though, will completely take you out of a round. Great touch is a little bit mysterious, but you can definitely train it and improve.

The core drill for putting is the ladder drill. The ladder drill is the putting-focused permutation of the Larry Bird drill. With your putts, it's much easier to hit the ball than your full golf swings, but putting demands greater focus to developing an incredibly sensitive and refined touch.

To do the ladder drill on the practice green, start out close to the hole and work your way out. Put tees in the ground at different distances and make five or ten putts from each one before you can progress to the next. Stand 3 feet from the hole, make three putts, move to 6 feet, repeat, then 9 feet. When you miss a putt, go back to the start. This can be torture when you're stuck out there endlessly, but it's a great way to learn to putt.

That said, some variability in touch can be even further refined. In the ladder drill, your putt can hit the hole and go in at a variety of speeds. Remove that tolerance from your training to improve further. As they say, aim small, miss small. I like to do a drill to get the ball past some point on the green but as close to the point as possible. You can do this with two balls. Hit one out a few feet, then hit the next one past it, but as close as possible to the first ball. Work these putts out longer until you hit long putts that die just as they roll past the other ball. If you master this practice, your feel on the greens will be exceptional.

LET THE BIG DOG EAT

READING GREENS

Master teacher that I am, all these skills I have given you are sadly moot if you cannot read a green. Reading greens is a fickle art that can be well developed and refined only with practice. From the start, you will probably have an instinct about how golf balls will break on greens (and that instinct is probably mostly right!), but here's some theory just so the devil doesn't say I left a base uncovered.

Greens have a "slope," meaning they're not flat but bumpy and often canted one way or another. Golf balls tend to roll downhill and follow this slope. If you hit a putt on a line and the green slopes to the left, the ball will turn to the left. If you hit a putt downhill, it will appear to roll faster than if you hit a putt on flat ground. Putting uphill, the putt will appear to roll slower than on flat greens. In cases of extreme slopes, the ball may actually accelerate downhill or turn around going uphill and come back.

In addition to slope, greens have what is known as "speed": the amount of resistance a green introduces to a golf ball's roll. On a shag carpet, your putting would go nowhere. In contrast, it would roll freely and nearly forever on a concrete floor. Putting greens are somewhere in between these two extremes but are all different from one another. Assessing their relative "speed" is required to inform the force you put into your putts and the break you read into them. In professional settings, green speeds are measured with a tool called a "Stimpmeter," which produces consistent readings of how far balls will tend to roll out. I don't think this is that important for reading greens yourself: after all, you won't be able to use the Stimp on each green before you putt, but it's worth knowing that higher Stimp numbers mean that the ball will roll out faster, and anything over a twelve is very fast.

Learning a green's speed is close to impossible in a vacuum. The best way to pick it up is (1) hit a series of putts on the practice green before your round (however, beware, practice greens are not always cut the same as competition greens); (2) watch your opponents' putts and chips to see how fast they roll, and (3) learn from the previous putts you have hit in a given round or on a given course.

This real-life lived experience will always be the best guide to understanding the speed of greens, but even absorbing all this, each green and each putt will nonetheless be different. So it's a good idea to be familiar with the cues that can affect green speed so that you can incorporate them into your mental model of each putt.

Begin with grass conditions. The shorter and smoother the cut of the green, the less rolling resistance the ball will experience and the freer it will roll. The type of grass matters too. Different types of grass have different characteristics, and different grasses at different courses have different characteristics. Hence the best way to read greens locally is just to go to the practice greens before every round and feel them out. However, practice greens are not always cut or maintained to the same speed and characteristics as the greens you will find on the course.

The firmness of the green and moisture on the green will also affect the rate at which a ball will slow down. When greens appear hard and burned out, they tend to roll faster. When they are wet, slower. Wind conditions will move a ball in motion, proportional to the strength of the wind. On a very windy day, this can dramatically change putts.

This is exacerbated by shade conditions. You should always expect a green in the sun to roll faster than one in the shade, but if the green in the sun drains poorly and is damp, this may not be the case.

Once you incorporate all of this, you will still have to account for the grain of the green, which is the direction the grass grows. This takes some practice to identify, though generally grass is shinier down grain. If you're putting into the grain, your putt will be slower and bumpier than with the grain, particularly if you're also going uphill.

This may be a lot to keep track of, but there are other idiosyncrasies that you should take into account in your putting. Even on greens that appear flat, putts will nonetheless tend to break with the underlying slope of the terrain. For instance, on mountain courses, putts will always tend to break down the mountain, even if the green appears flat. Similarly, putts always tend to break toward large bodies of water. These effects can be subtle, but to putt truly well, you should incorporate all of them into your reads.

This may sound like an impossible set of criteria to internalize, and on some level, it is. Nobody consciously thinks about all these things before each putt. Bryson claims to, but there is reason for skepticism. Instead, knowing these things, understanding them intuitively, and experiencing them firsthand will help you incorporate them into a holistic understanding of your putt. There's no objective way to measure what a putt will do before you hit it. Your understanding is subjective; through practice, you refine it as your estimates asymptotically approach truth.

In addition to developing this holistic understanding, certain pieces of the process are fundamental to consistently reading greens well. The first and most valuable practice is watching other players' putts and chips. This is the only opportunity you will get in the course of play to observe an objective measure of the green's slope and speed.

You are not allowed to roll balls on the green to gauge slope other than in the course of play. To do so furtively is against the rules and cheating. Other people's balls, on the other hand, are fair game. If someone is putting along a similar line as you, make sure that before they putt, you stand in a location where you can watch their ball roll. Don't stand too close to the other player; you have to be respect-ful. But as soon as they hit that ball, walk behind them and watch that baby move. Good players will make many more long putts after seeing another player's putt roll on a similar line. PGA pros make something like 95% of 10-footers after watching someone else putt. Look it up. You should always be on the lookout for opportunities to do this in the course of play. You might save yourself a stroke or two a round.

Sometimes you won't have this opportunity, though, and you still need process. For me, the most important part of this process is marking the ball, picking it up, and then proceeding to look at the putt from all four sides. This approach will give you a far more robust understanding of all the conditions I described above than a simple glance. It's not always an obvious practice, though! Something like 85% of the time, at first glance, a good golfer could correctly read a putt without looking at it closely. You have to resist this urge. If you don't, your initial read is wrong 15% of the time, and you will kick yourself.

Here's the process I follow. When it comes time to putt, after you mark your ball, get low to the ground[66] and look down the line of the putt toward the hole. After this, walk to the other side of the ball and repeat the process. As you walk around the hole, look at the line of your putt from the left and the right. I find it helpful to get at least one look at the putt from relatively far away. (You should have already been looking at the putt as you walk up to the green.) Through all of this, you're trying to determine the direction of the break, and maybe more important, whether the putt is uphill or downhill and by how much.

Almost all of my three-putts could have been avoided with a look at the putt from all four sides. This exercise often reveals something (for me, probably that it was uphill or downhill) that I didn't pick up on the initial read. I have missed many putts stupidly because I didn't follow this process. Each time you avoid a three-or-more putt, you're saving strokes. There are very few strokes you will find out

---

66 However you are able to, given your level of flexibility. We are not all of us Camilo Villegas, and I struggle with getting down sometimes if I'm injured. But really, the closer to the ground, the better.

there on the course more easily than the handful that you can save just by following a simple green-reading process.

FINAL THOUGHTS ON PUTTING

Even with all these tools of learning to putt straight, developing feel, and reading greens, you probably won't putt all that well at first. You have to practice. A lot. Once you can hit the ball well, good putting will unlock good scoring. Nothing gets a round going like making long putts or saving par with a 5-footer.

In this section, I have repeatedly emphasized strategies to get the ball close to the hole and avoid three-putts. This is sound advice, as you cannot play good golf and three-putt. Great putting demands more, though. Great players make birdie putts in bunches. This is a function of the accretion of all the skills described above, but it's also a mindset. Every time a great putter approaches the ball and looks at the hole, they imagine that ball dropping in. Learn this mindset and hunt for birds, and you will find yourself scoring much better.[67]

I talk about the mental aspect of scoring in the next chapter but know now that much of the war of golf is fought inside your head. Your practice should be tailored to growing your skills, yes, but you should also increase your confidence. When a golfer is confident,

---

67 Some people also say that when you find a feather in the fairway, you should plant it upright. Planting feathers, growing birdies. Hard to say if this is true or not.

they say the hole looks like a trash can. When they have lost their confidence, it looks like a pinprick.

One other stray note to internalize.

Mid- to high-handicap players have a tendency to leave putts short. In a way, this is safe, as there's less risk short than long. Short putts, however, are death, as you will never make them. In a very literal sense, putts that stop rolling short of the hole will never fall into the hole, whereas putts that blow 5 feet by the hole sometimes will. For this reason, you should endeavor to never leave a putt short. Internalize the old golf saying "Never up, never down" to remember this before each putt. This practice will help you avoid hearing the equally prevalent invective "you fucking coward," shouted by weak-kneed putters worldwide after their balls wind up short of the hole.

Similar sage wisdom applies to the side of the hole you miss on. Missing putts on the high side—in other words, reading too much break into a putt so that the ball doesn't quite break all the way to the hole—is preferable to missing on the low side. Low-side misses never have a chance, and if they happen to catch the edge of the cup, they will have less purchase to potentially wobble in. On the other hand, high-side misses can take the slope of the green in, and if they happen to catch an edge, they're more likely to fall.

Take all this advice, practice often, read your putts from all four sides, go long, go high, and you will start making birdies and avoiding three-putts. That is good because now it's time to discuss scoring.

CHAPTER 7

SCORING

Scoring is weird. Extreme talent in any one facet of the game cannot, on its own, make a golfer a good scorer. Even players who are very good in multiple areas of the game may not consistently score well. And yet, on any golf course, you'll be able to find several golfers who don't seem to be exceptionally good at any aspect of the game yet score extremely well. These people will beat you. It will be very annoying. You see them again and again. The scrappy old-timer who can't hit the ball much past 200 yards and hits hybrids into greens but keeps coming up with pars and clutch birdies. The former hockey player with the weird swing who shanks chips but is still out there breaking 80. These players are everywhere. People who just have an instinct to score.

I propose to you here that scoring is more than the sum of its parts. Oddly, scoring is a skill on its own. Of course, having skill in each area of the game positions a player to score, but these skills won't make good scores on their own. Skill has to be applied in the right sequence, with a strategy, and without catastrophic error. This can all be learned.

In my years of trying to understand why some people score as well (or as badly) as they do, I have come to understand the "scoring" skill as having two primary facets. These elements are related yet also in tension. The first one is avoiding blowups, and the second is finding birdies. They're related because, in either case, they will be undermined by uncontrolled nerves and emotions. You have to learn to control those impulses.

However, these elements are also fundamentally distinct because one counsels caution and the other risk-taking. A more aggressive style of play will put you in danger of blowup but also may yield more birdies. Resolving this tension is highly individual and, in my view, best informed by the relative skill level of each golfer. The better you are, the more risk you can take. Great golfers find the perfect balance of both.

Of the two skills, avoiding blowups is the more important. Many golfers ruin hole after hole, round after round, with poor planning and big numbers. It is the particular cruelty of golf that every shot must count, and you must live with every one of your mistakes. These mistakes have a fundamental tendency to compound and create even more difficult shots, then more mistakes, and so on. Every golfer must strategize around avoiding these kinds of compounding errors to play good golf, which involves control of the golf ball and planning. This, in turn, takes emotional regulation and acceptance of hard choices under pressure.

The nose for birdies is the ancillary skill. While a player who frequently blows up will never be able to overcome that with birdies, players who know how to make birdies and frequently do are massively advantaged over those who fear the bird. This skill comes from planning and strategy, but self-belief is a crucial predicate.[68] Most of us golfers don't see ourselves as the kind of player who makes a lot of birdies, and so we subtly sabotage ourselves to manifest this self-belief. Learning to make birdies, then, is not just the accretion of the physical skills of a golfer but a battle fought in your mind. Once you believe that you're a player making birdies, I guarantee that you'll see many more rolling in.

While these skills are mental, you should note that they tend to align with some of the physical abilities I described above. Blowups tend to come on full swings when players put the ball dramatically out of play (though not always). Birdies tend to come with the flat stick (though, again, not always). You can learn both of these skills in concert, as they are internally consistent with each other. But I suggest that most golfers focus on removing blowups first because these are devastating to a round and can completely derail the birdie train. As I say, ball-striking is more important than putting. To the extent that you have to focus on one and not the other, avoiding blowups should come before the birdie nose.

---

68 This is Bob Rotella's idea, not mine. Shout out to Dr. Bob. Buy yourself a copy of *Golf Is Not a Game of Perfect*.

AVOIDING BLOWUPS

The first key to avoiding blowups is strategy. Know where you cannot hit the ball. When I stand up to a tee on any golf hole and begin to plan my shot, I first figure out where the ball will be dead. By "dead" I mean any spot on the course where you will not be able to play your next shot toward the hole. These are the spots from where you will have to take a penalty or play sideways to continue. Hitting the ball dead will cost you one, two, or even three strokes. The most important part of every tee shot is hitting your ball somewhere where it will not be dead.

Now I don't want to trigger you, but it's probably helpful for some of you to consider just what impediments off the tee might make your ball dead. Things that might make your ball dead include the following horrors.

DEEP SHRUBBERY, ROCKY TERRAIN, GORSE, OR OTHER IMPEDIMENTS THAT WILL MAKE YOUR BALL IMPOSSIBLE TO FIND. A lost ball will cost you a stroke and distance. If you haven't hit a provisional, you will have to return to the tee, which you probably won't do. So this resting place for your ball is the most dire because it'll take you completely out of the hole in match play and poison your scorecard in stroke play.

OUT OF BOUNDS. This has all the disadvantages of deep shrubbery or badlands, in that you will lose stroke and distance, but has the very minor advantage of being identifiable from the tee. At least you will probably hit a provisional and avoid completely fucking yourself.[69] Nonetheless, endeavor to not hit the ball out of bounds.

WATER WITHOUT CROSSING LAND. If you hit the ball in the water and your ball doesn't cross land first, you have to re-tee or tee off from the drop zone, losing stroke and at least some distance.

WATER AFTER CROSSING LAND. You don't lose your distance (or as much of it), but you do have to drop, potentially in some unfortunate turf. Hitting the ball in the water occasionally will not ruin your round if you're mentally stable, but it's still really bad.

MARKED HAZARDS. Hazards carry most of the problems of water and, again, do not penalize distance, only stroke, but have a slight advantage over water, sometimes permitting a ball to be found and played without penalty.

EXTREMELY PENAL LIES. These include deep rough, very deep bunkers, groves of trees that might obstruct your shot to the green, or any other severe impediment. These scenarios are very penal, but not quite as much as the ones described above.

All these outcomes should be avoided if you want to play good golf. This may seem difficult if you're spraying the ball all over the

---

69 I was playing a competitive match with a stranger at a course called Sable Oaks (sadly, it was bulldozed a few years back). I hit a bomb drive that rolled slightly onto an adjacent fairway. When we got there, my competitor gleefully informed me that hitting it into the wrong fairway was out of bounds. I checked and old Sable did try to enforce this dumbass rule. The USGA defines out of bounds as being off the golf course's property, so if a course or a competitor tries to enforce this kind of in-course out of bounds against you, tell them to go fuck themselves. If a course insists on creating this in-course out of bounds, leave. Play another course, finish your round, go to the bar, order a nice cold beer and a burger, then call the first course and tell them to go fuck themselves.

course and hardly know where you will hit it, but I have a secret that will help: aim away from the shit. In general, your ball will go in the direction you aim your body at address. This means that even when you spray the ball, you can still reliably control its direction from the tee. All you gotta do is turn away from the bad stuff!

Even on difficult courses, most holes will have truly penal trouble only on one side or the other of the fairway. Aiming your body away from the bad side and toward the good side is easy. No matter how egregiously you slice the ball, if you're aimed at a 50-degree angle away from the trouble right, you are not going to slice it into that trouble very often.

This strategy is further strengthened by using the whole tee box to aim away from trouble with even more dramatic angles. I cannot tell you how many people I have seen aim their bodies directly out of bounds and hit the ball straight where they were aiming. Most of the time, these lost souls then become angry or bewildered while I gently try to explain their folly. Don't be like them. If you aim away from the trouble, you usually won't hit it there, I promise you.

At first, applying this strategy, you may feel like you're not giving yourself good positions off the tee. Crucially, though, you will be consistently in better positions off the tee where you can take your second shot toward the hole. This is far from a given in the world of amateur golf, and practicing this will put you at an immediate advantage over many others!

Remember, getting your ball in play is the most important priority for the tee shot. Hitting three out of four tee shots perfectly and the fourth out of bounds is far worse than hitting four tee shots that were only 80% perfect. What's more, as you improve your shotmaking, you can safely take less severe angles away from the trouble or even take it on from time to time (although I would counsel against this if you can avoid it). This kind of risk management off the tee is the first step to avoiding fucking up your rounds; the next step comes on your second shot.

SECOND SHOT

So now you've successfully gotten off the tee, and your ball is in play. Congratulations! You get a gold star. Now you're standing at your ball for your second shot. You must again make the same risk management calculation you just made off the tee.

Maybe you're dead center of the fairway. In that case, all the risk you must consider is the danger around your target. Is short of the green dead? Long of the green? Your first question still must be where you cannot hit the ball. The farther you are from the green, the greater the area potentially in play for your second shot. Taken to the extreme, if you have a long iron or fairway wood in hand, I would suggest a similar risk management strategy as you use from the tee. You're probably not much more accurate with those clubs than you would be with your driver.

Approaching the green, distance control becomes extremely important. While most tee shots can safely land anywhere in large areas and have relatively comfortable margins for error, greens are not as forgiving. You have to figure out if short or long of the green is dead and tailor your shot to get your ball to the correct distance. Green complexes are frequently also more difficult on one side or the other. For instance, deep bunkering may be placed to the right or left of the flag, and this should be avoided. It's also far better to be below the hole and chip up to it than to be above it. Often, there's water around the green. Consider all this and choose the most aggressive shot you can confidently make while *avoiding* trouble.[70] A misplaced approach shot can easily turn a great tee shot into a double bogey. Persistent mistakes here will surely take you out of a round.

In addition to these concerns about the dead zone, on your second shot, you should also consider issues of lie and impediment. If you're hitting over or under trees, as I mentioned in the trajectory section above, your first priority has to be not hitting those trees. Whenever you find yourself in that situation, your priority is to give yourself enough loft to get over the trees or a low-enough lofted club to slap under the trees. You also must remember not to aim close to the trunks of trees. These shots are difficult, and you want to give yourself as much margin for error as possible. You will always make mistakes; good strategy prevents those mistakes from turning into big scores. It's a disaster to hit a tree and fail to improve your position; this kind of error puts you at risk of double bogey or worse.

Sometimes your percentage of avoiding a tree is so low that you have no safe avenue to escape forward. When this happens, you

---

70 Note that sometimes there truly is no trouble around the green, and you should welcome this as a green light to take dead aim.

LET THE BIG DOG EAT

must hit the ball out sideways. This is known in the business as "taking your medicine." Playing golf, I have seen novices repeatedly play straight at trees to try to go at the green, only to watch their ball hit wood and bounce back. I'll tell them, "You have to play sideways," and hear back, "I see a hole." This is dumb. Take your goddamn medicine. You don't appear brave. You look like an idiot. When your only shot is to punch out sideways, that is your only shot.

Note that if you become highly skilled, you can take more risks safely. I play through trees all the time and rarely hit them. The old adage is true, trees are indeed 90% air. The difference between me taking on these shots and most golfers (probably including you) is that I can manage the risk while making aggressive plays because I have hit these shots thousands of times and am confident that I can get the ball moving exactly on line. You have to assess your skill level, and if you can't say the same about yourself, you will *play better golf* by taking your medicine when your lie demands it.

The same risk management strategies apply in other situations: deep rough, deep bunkers, bad turf, and so on. Suppose there is a chance you won't be able to meaningfully advance the ball out of these dire conditions. In that case, your first priority must be to do all you can to put yourself back in play. If you can manage to do this effectively while prioritizing identifying and avoiding dead zones, you will rarely make worse than bogey.

The first barrier to applying this strategy is a lack of knowledge. That's a big part of why I wrote this book: I see so many players who have never been exposed to the knowledge necessary to make good strategic choices on the golf course. Well, lucky you, now you've read my advice and know how to make these choices well. However, in my opinion, that leaves the second major barrier and the more pernicious of the two. This barrier is in your mind. You must always *choose* to apply the lessons of risk management in your own game.

This mental fortitude is the key to playing good golf. You have to be able to buckle down and play the right shot, even when you're frustrated and angry.

After a bad shot, most players get frustrated. I've watched many angry players do something dumb immediately after they put themselves out of position from the tee. Remember that you can only rarely save a stroke with a spectacular shot. But you can easily lose two with a bad one. I won't pretend to be immune to this impulse. I've compounded many errors in my day. When I learned not to, though, I became a much stronger golfer. To play great golf, you must maintain calm and play analytically from tee to green.

The first step to doing this is simple. You just have to know and acknowledge that you should play this way. Say it to yourself, write it down, and tell a friend. Commit on some level to this strategic approach. This will give you a solid foundation when it's hard to maintain focus on the course.

If you believe me and buy that you should stay calm and play analytically, the next step is to *try* to do it. For some people, this will be easy. Some people (not me) are instinctually levelheaded and can execute a plan once they know what it is. Many, though, will struggle. Now that you know what to do, consider the emotions that might lead you astray.

Controlling your emotions is one of the central challenges a golfer faces. This challenge can't be faced simply with resolve, but it should be actively supported with off-course practice and mindful effort. I find meditation extremely useful for identifying physical cues to emotional states and the role that emotions play in my life. This self-knowledge is invaluable in the golf game, so I would advise any golfer to meditate. Considering what other inputs affect your golf game is also a good idea. Caffeine has been shown to improve focus. I always try to consume at least 200 mg of caffeine before I play any competitive round. If this makes you jittery, consider consuming tea or yerba mate, which also contains L-theanine, the consumption of which, alongside caffeine, should reduce the jittery feeling.

You should eat too! Emotional volatility seems to me to increase dramatically as blood glucose levels drop. While a round of golf may not seem like a strenuous physical activity, you are moving your body for what is often well over four hours. This is guaranteed to lower your blood glucose levels and adversely affect your play on the back nine. For this reason, I recommend eating carbohydrates throughout your round to keep your mind and body sharp. Alcohol can reduce focus, but beer can also serve as this carbohydrate for you drinkers out there. In this way, beer drinking might actually benefit some golfers. For more discussion on drinking during a round, see chapter 9 on consumption norms in golf.

Mindfulness, then, in your preparations and the things you consume is the best technique to build mental fortitude. Combine this with the strategy I taught you above and some practice, and you will avoid many blowups out on the course that would once have been your hobgoblin. By doing this, you may save five, six, or seven strokes a round. That is serious stuff and will change your strata as a golfer. Now to consider the other side of the scoring coin, making birdies.

HUNTING BIRDIES

To make birdies, you have to do everything right. First, you must hit a strong tee shot. You can only rarely birdie from the tee, but you can always lose one. Next, you must get your approach shot somewhere on the green, preferably somewhere close. If you leave yourself somewhere bad, you have no chance at birdie. Finally, you have to make a putt.

Making birdies really requires all facets of your golf game to work in harmony. However, there are three skills of particular importance. In reverse order of importance, these are (1) driving distance, (2) approach shot accuracy, and (3) putting.

Driving distance is straightforward. I've already told you that you must hit your tee shots in a good position to make birdies. Applying that constraint, the farther you hit the ball, the easier it will be to put your approach shots on the green and close to the hole. If you can hit the ball farther without sacrificing much accuracy, you should. In fact, if you can hit the ball much farther, even at the expense of sacrificing a lot of accuracy, it may still make sense. I already told you about hitting it hard. Being in the rough 50 yards from the green may be a much easier shot than being in the fairway from 150 yards, but this will depend on you and your game. When you get the chance, let the big dog eat.

Second, approach shots. This, too, does not involve anything too complicated. Shots outside a range of perhaps 120 yards are never reliably placed in prime scoring position. But when you do find yourself with a wedge in hand, you have an opportunity to take dead aim. Doing this consistently and accurately will produce more birdies. Your scoring clubs can be drilled down and finessed through careful practice. Practice until you can drop a ball in a bucket with a sand wedge from 80 yards, and you will have the skill to prosper. I'll tell you more about how to make the most of your practice time a little later in this book.

None of that matters for shit, however, if you don't drain birdie putts. This is the core skill that leads to more birdies. It's not just being a better putter overall. Improving your precision without making more putts will do you no good here; you need to buckle down and knock the ball into the cup. To do that, you'll have to be able to look at the putt and want the birdie more than you fear hitting a 5-foot comeback putt to the hole.[71]

All the putting techniques I told you above also apply to putting for birdies. Part of the process will always be the slow refinement of

---

[71] Never fear the comebacker.

narrowing the variance in your stroke, making smaller and smaller misses as you improve. This, however, is not sufficient on its own to master the skill of making birdies. There's a mental switch that must flip, and once it does, it will open up the whole world of competitive golf.[72] I wish I had a secret key to teach you to make birdies, but I have none. For me, there's a certain threshold of confidence. Once I pass it, I pour them in. Getting there is the hard part.

There is one drill I like for making birdies. Go to your home course and play from the farthest tees up,[73] play eighteen holes, and focus on making as many birdies as possible. While we may get only a few opportunities to look at a birdie from 6,800 yards, playing from 5,200 gives us many more, perhaps as many as ten or fifteen a round. Having all these opportunities grants you the ability to take birdie putts repeatedly. This helps you simulate the pressure you will inevitably feel over the ball during competition. It will also help you taste the joy of watching the ball go in. You get used to making birdies, and the next thing you know, you believe that you are a person who makes birdies. I suggest playing this way often if you have the opportunity.

---

72 Interestingly, research has shown that for equivalent putts for par and birdie, golfers are more likely to make the pars. My law school professor Cass Sunstein takes this as an indication of *loss aversion*, a manifestation of the human tendency to experience diminishing marginal returns. I think most golfers are just afraid to be great.

73 If you're a woman and you already play from the farthest tees up, apologies that this drill is a little trickier for you. There's no reason you can't get the same training, however, by just walking 100 yards in front of your tees and starting there. You want to make the hole easy for yourself, so all you have to worry about is draining birds.

Your mind will be the ultimate battlefield in scoring. You have to be able to see yourself draining the putt, bombing the drive, and flopping the wedge *before* you can manifest it in your own game. We have all seen players who stroke the ball on the practice range, then get out on the course and collapse. Most of us can make 5-foot putts on the practice green all day, but our knees will start to shake during a competition when we see that we have left ourselves a short slippery one. Everyone feels this, and the dedicated effort to control these feelings makes great golfers great. You are not simply born with a strong mind; you must commit to making your mind strong. This comes from the drills to see yourself rolling birdies in. It comes from meditating off the course to control your emotions after a bad shot.

All of us have birdie looks. All of us hit bad shots. What will you do in these situations? This is the question golf asks you about yourself. It's a mistake to think that the answer is static. You have a life to build the answer again and again. This game will keep asking you. So don't ask for whom the bell tolls. It tolls for thee. Stand up and score.

CHAPTER 8

PRACTICING

YOU CAN'T PLAY GOLF WELL IF YOU DON'T PRACTICE. I WOULD WARN you that this will be hard work, but if you have the time and space in your life to devote to practicing golf, you should really consider how lucky you are indeed. I have always found practicing golf a joy. If you care about getting better and have time to spend at the practice range, the hard work is not in making the swings or stroking the putts. The hard work of practicing golf is mustering the discipline and knowledge to do it well. You're already a step ahead because you're reading this book, but the discipline you will need has to come from within.

It's extremely tempting to go to the range and bang out a bucket of balls to release some tension. At Purpoodock growing up, I remember watching players do this *every day* after work for years and years without ever getting any better. It was so baffling to me.

I couldn't understand why they were willing to put in the time, but not the focus, to improve. Mindless repetition may have its place early in the learning curve, but after a certain point on your golf journey, it will be mindful practice that actual moves the needle.

We all naturally do what is comfortable to us, so we have to do something uncomfortable to change our patterns and improve. Some limited gains are available to novice golfers from simple, repetitive movements. Once you have built a basic swing, though, and you can hit a ball somewhat consistently, you will have to make a focused effort to improve your game. This probably sounds easy to you, but I promise it is not.

It takes real commitment to maintain focus and practice a single element of your swing or stroke. It takes uncommon insight to identify your problems and courage to change them. As you grow this way, you won't see the reward of your efforts for a long time.

Every swing change you make will be uncomfortable initially and likely produce some terrible shots as you try it out. Sticking with it will take faith that these swing changes will accumulate into improvements over time.

If you leave an empty cup under a leaky faucet, not much will happen at first. But if you leave it there overnight and return the next day, the cup will run over. Remember this as you practice golf. From small things, big things one day come. Make a plan and stick to it. You can't do it all at once. Slowly is the only way you will ever become a good golfer.

PRACTICE STRATEGIES FOR NOVICE GOLFERS

When you first learn to play golf, I give you license to bang away at the ball as much as you want. In this stage, I think most learning comes from repetition. For instance, you're learning to deliver a clubhead to the golf ball. This comes from a kind of neuromuscular connection that I believe is developed naturally from repeating the motion.

It's okay if your early practice is not absolutely laser-focused all the time because you're learning the fundamental aspect of ball-striking—striking the ball. You probably don't have the coordination or flexibility to make the sort of complex motions necessary to execute high-level golf shots yet, anyway. This means, as a novice, your practice is mainly about getting in many reps. That doesn't mean you should not be mindful, though! Control the things you can.

What you can control from the very beginning is your setup. There is no excuse for neglecting it. To me, careful attention to setup during practice sessions is a must. It should be rigorously adhered to by golfers of all skill levels all the time. Always practice shots with alignment tools on the ground. Always be mindful of your posture and head position. Pick a grip and always practice with it.

As I stated above in the setup chapter, your setup must be drilled into your brain so firmly that it's second nature: that's how to build a setup that will stand up under pressure. These moments on the range, your practice, are the only chances you have to build that routine.

Even as a novice, you should always carry two surveying sticks and use them when you practice. Practicing with alignment tools will help you standardize your setup to later withstand pressure and provide you with much more accurate feedback for your shots. Likely, as a novice, you have no idea where the ball will go when you hit it. Using a stick as an aiming tool, you are committed to a target, and if your ball doesn't go toward it, you know you hit it wrong. Without a solid reference point for your aim, you may not be able to consistently identify your own errors. Get some sticks!

This is a good juncture to discuss aim in general. You should always pick a target. Every shot you hit in competition. Every shot you hit in practice. The target should not be a broad area but something distinct. I usually use the top of a tree (as in, a single branch) behind my intended target because I find these easy to isolate against the backdrop of the sky. It allows me to be extremely specific in my start line.[74] Practicing on ranges, you will be graced with a whole menagerie of intermediate targets scattered across the range. Pick one as a target and aim your stick down the barrel. Once you have your stick down and alignment set, you can work through your clubs along the same line, starting in front of the target and going deeper and deeper down range as you use longer clubs.

---

74 Because of this, I often struggle to find target lines and get my ball moving toward the hole on links courses without many trees. This perhaps advocates for a different aiming convention. Make your own up, I don't think it matters very much what it is, just that it's specific and you're comfortable with it.

LET THE BIG DOG EAT

Generally, I think it's not good practice to aim at those ball-picking golf carts that pimply teenagers drive around ranges. These carts are moving, after all, and your golf targets never will be. It is a good sport, though.[75]

The same advice on alignment with the full swing also goes for putting and chipping. Make sure that you control what you can in your practice but give yourself the freedom to practice for volume over quality and experiment. Feel okay pouring the balls into the cup. Get a feel for a crispy little chip shot and get used to seeing the ball go in the hole. If you give significant time to these parts of your game, you will see dividends fairly quickly, as they're easier to attain basic mastery in rather than in the full swing. In either case, once you're competent at these skills, you become an intermediate, and your practice routines should change accordingly.

PRACTICE STRATEGIES FOR INTERMEDIATE GOLFERS

Felicitations! You are an intermediate golfer. This means that you make some pars in every round, you can generally hit the ball where you want, and occasionally drain a putt. You probably also have some catastrophic flaws in your game that consistently take you out of holes, and sometimes you screw things up for no reason at all. This,

---

75 This is a joke. Don't roast some poor teenager picking balls on the range.

sadly, is golf.[76] Your practice strategies should now reflect that you have a grasp of the basics. You likely will no longer benefit from just whacking balls without any plan. Now you have to use your mind.

As an intermediate golfer, you should start training yourself to hit different kinds of shots. This will develop the tools you can use to hone your abilities as an advanced golfer. By developing a feel for different swing changes, you can understand the results those changes will produce on the course.

When you stand up to the ball, instead of trying to just whack it, work on each of your shots in succession. Hit the ball high, hit it low, hit draws, hit cuts. Remember that you always want the ball to start on your target line, but that line need not be in alignment with your body. For me, my cuts always start right, so I build that in when I'm planning my shots.

"But, Aaron. I don't know how to hit any of those shots." Fear not, peasants; you can always refer to my chapter on the swing in the spin section to guide you. Ultimately, though, these shots are based on feels. You can and should use a guide like mine, or a friend or mentor, to learn the swing feel to make the ball move initially. But once you have a kernel of an idea, only the repetition and practice

---

76 I say "sadly" half-jokingly here. The difficulty of golf is actually what makes it such a joyful game. It can never be truly mastered, yet improvement is always available to us with focused effort. In this way, it may bring us joy through life, unlike false idols like wealth and beauty. As long as we have strength in our body to grip the club and swing, we can keep working on our game. On a darker note, I have heard it suggested that the randomness of the game lends it a casino-like quality. This might contribute to its addictive nature.

LET THE BIG DOG EAT

of those techniques and their refinement will teach you to work the ball in different ways.

You should also be practicing your distance control at this stage. The Larry Bird drill can come in handy here. Get a feel for how to hit your clubs to different distances, and you will be in a much stronger position to fill in the gaps in your shot distances.

Speaking of which, now that you're hitting your clubs relatively consistently, it's time to learn the distances you hit each of them. This is called gapping, and it's a fundamental aspect of learning to play golf. For each of your clubs and for each shot, you are comfortable playing with those clubs. You shouldn't just know a single number. You should know at least three: how far you hit the ball stock, hard, and mishit. You should know how far your ball can travel in the air and how far it will roll after hitting the ground. This probably sounds like a lot to know, and it is! But after playing for a while, it will be like the back of your hand.

I gotta be honest; I don't regap my clubs regularly. I just know how far each of them goes from hitting them all the time. That's possible for me because I built a baseline earlier in my life. Now, I can just modify that baseline when something changes and start hitting the ball to different distances. You will probably have to go through the arduous process of actually writing down and internalizing all your distances.

You must know these distances, including and especially carry distance and mishit carry distance. To avoid obstacles, you have to consistently take enough club to carry over the obstacle even on a mishit.

You, as an intermediate golfer, may be prone to some vanity. You probably think that you hit the ball farther than you actually do. Consequently, when gapping your clubs, I recommend developing an objective measure of how far you're hitting the ball. If you're broke, you can go out there and pace off your shots. If you can afford it, though, it's easier to drop the coin for a Trackman[77] session to really dial in these numbers. Without an objective measure of your shots (be it pacing, targets, or the Trackman), you will lie to yourself, and lying to yourself usually doesn't make you a better golfer.

As an intermediate, in addition to learning these different shot shapes and distances, you should also be drilling your chipping and putting. Practice chipping from different surfaces, sand, tall grass, and tight lies. Make sure you stretch out your skills and become comfortable taking these shots in all kinds of different places. Use the chipping tricks I told you about in that chapter. For putting, focus on seeing the ball go in the hole, practice from different angles and distances.

A *major key* in practicing putting is ensuring that the ball always starts on your line. Feel is so important, but as the saying goes, you have to marry the line and speed. If you don't know what line your putt will go on, you don't stand much chance of getting it right very

---

77 Note that as of 2024, Trackman is state of the art. If this kind of tracking becomes cheaper or easier to access in the future, as I have no doubt it will, it may merit earlier inclusion in practice regimens.

often. I have a couple of drills to really nail down the direction of your putts. First, find some straight putt, and down some straight line (I like a surveying stick, but some people use a tool that places a chalk line on the practice green or something else similar). Now hit your putt and ensure that it tracks the straight line every time. I like this drill in concept, but practically, I don't think it works perfectly. Once you take the alignment tool away with the putter, your head starts to spin on your shoulders, and you lose feel. To be clear, I think this drill is better than nothing and is good to get a feel. The second drill, though, I think is even better.

Put your ball on the ground and line up your putter head behind the ball so that a straight putt will go in the hole (I like this drill from about 10 feet). Use two tees to set up a little gate just wider than your putter head. Now, when you hit the putt, your putter must pass through this little gate, standardizing your stroke. Hit a few like that till you have a feel for the ball rolling in the hole. Now create intermediate gates, slightly wider than a ball, on the path between the ball and the hole. Now, when you putt, the ball must pass through every gate to get to the hole. If you miss left or right, you will hit a tee and know immediately what happened. To putt well, you should absolutely drill this down. Do it every day you practice, even if only for fifteen minutes, and I promise your putting will improve.[78]

---

[78] One note on putting: when you practice, the only makes that count are dead center of the hole. You might get lucky in your round and squeak one in the side, but when we practice, dead center is all that counts. Aim small, miss small.

Doing all that, you should be shot-shaping and draining putts. You should be able to chip effectively from all surfaces and know how far you hit the ball. With all these skills in your arsenal, you should be scoring better. Score better for long enough, and you will eventually become an advanced golfer. This is where the really hard part starts.

PRACTICE STRATEGIES FOR ADVANCED GOLFERS

If you're an advanced golfer, congratulations. It's often said that golf is more fun shooting in the 80s than in the 90s, and even more fun in the 70s than in the 80s. Wherever you are, you've acquired the skills to intentionally direct your ball in the way you want and, in turn, put it into the hole. This, in effect, gives you the ability to play golf and not just slap it around. This, however, is where improvement will become markedly more difficult and take more focused and intentional work on your part. It takes time to refine your swing and iron out flaws, which can be frustrating. You won't see progress in real-time, and the efficacy of the steps you take will only be apparent in retrospect. In this way, golf mirrors life.

My first piece of advice to the advanced golfer is to buy a tripod and use it to record your practice sessions. Tripods cost something like $15 on Amazon and fold up small enough to fit in your bag. If you have an iPhone (and if you don't, miss me with those green texts), you can record your swing in slow motion and get a slowed-down view of the entire move. Using a Trackman with the video is even better. It will give you an even clearer view, but, as I said, the tripod costs fifteen dollars, and a Trackman costs something like thirty thousand dollars, so I'd start with the tripod.

Armed with your camera and your sticks, you have all the tools to evaluate your swing freshly. This self-evaluation doesn't actually start with the camera (I just want you to be prepared). Rather, the first step is to take inventory of your mishits and missed shots. What patterns do you see?

Flaws in your swing will manifest; first, in the contact you're making with the ball; second, in the direction you're hitting the ball (relative to your intended target line); and third, in the spin you put on the ball (relative to the spin you intended). If you're like me, you will have issues with all these metrics and in every direction from time to time, but the purpose of evaluation is to identify trends. What mistakes do you keep making over and over again?

Poor contact can arise from many errors. Pretty much any strike of the ball that isn't on the center of the clubface will produce a mishit that will reduce the distance the ball flies and may change its direction. Balls low on the face will come out low and hot; if they're very low on the face, they may be skulled. Balls high on the face will balloon high and short. Too far to the inside or outside of the club-face, you will feel a ringing in your hand, hear a clank, and see your ball gently tumbling in the wrong direction. The extreme of any of these can be a shank, top, or dead miss. Balls that would be high on the face on the tee may be chunks off the turf, and dribble in front of you, so consider that when evaluating your contact. Don't take this list as fully inclusive of mishits, either.

Poor direction relative to alignment is caused by your clubface being open or closed (again relative to your target line) at impact. This may be caused by a grip being too strong or weak or your club path not aligning with your body, causing it to swing in a different direction and take the clubhead with it.

Finally, spin problems are caused by your clubhead path being from the outside or the inside of the angle of the clubface. This could manifest as shots that start right then go right, the big slice for a right-handed golfer, or the opposite, shots starting left and going left. On the other hand, your initial direction may be right, only to swerve away from your target from an incorrect spin. Maybe your ball comes out left and then spins right—this might be a pretty handy shot. Take inventory of it, nonetheless!

There are a lot of ways to fuck up. This means you'll probably be unable to figure out your errors in one swing or even one session. Over time, consider what you're doing over and over again and think about what the clubhead must be doing at impact to cause those errors. If this isn't working, look online and see what others say about your mishits. Go to a friend or coach! Sometimes another voice is valuable here. Just be aware that your swing is your own. I've often found that others are as likely as not to give me advice that actively hurts my swing.

LET THE BIG DOG EAT

Your goal as an advanced golfer is to decipher the information available to you to understand which of these issues is holding back your game. You might be able to tell just from hitting shots and watching where they end up. If you hit big draws that miss your targets left consistently, that's easy to identify. However, most of your swing flaws will not be so obvious. For any of these issues, there are usually multiple swing problems that could be causing them. And you, feeble-minded and helpless, are woefully undermatched to the task of identifying them by feel. This is where your sticks and your camera come in.

My impression in my years of playing and practicing golf has been that we cannot feel our swings. "But, Papa Brogs," you say, "I can feel my swing; that's how I do it, and I feel the changes I want to make. That's what you told me to do!" What did I tell you? You do feel your swing happening, which allows you to initiate your move and manipulate your shotmaking, but what you feel is not an accurate mental model of your actual swing.

Remember what I told you about Jim Furyk? That he didn't know his swing was weird until he was on TV? That's what I mean. When you swing, you feel what you're doing, but that feeling doesn't give you any feedback on whether your swing is closer to a productive swing. In fact, swing changes that will improve your swing will feel bad when you implement them. This is because your "feel" is about reproducing what your body is comfortable with. A swing change necessarily moves away from that to achieve something else. Swing changes are supposed to feel weird. If you want to improve, you must internalize and accept that fact. If you believe me about this, you will understand the following corollary. You can't use feel as your guide in improving. You need objective measures.

Your first objective measure is the sensation of contact in your hands.[79] You may not be able to tell what your motion is in an absolute sense, but you can tell what kind of contact you're making with the ball. Consider how your contact varies from the ideal, dead-center strike. Second, as an objective measure, you can assess where the ball goes. However, as I've said repeatedly, this is possible only if you standardize your alignment first. As your third measure, you can use video to guide your swing and correct its potential flaws. Any one of these alone cannot give you the full picture of your swing. But they can be used concurrently to holistically understand the shortcomings of your move. A Trackman or other swing-tracking tool can be used to go into further detail, but it shouldn't substitute for these core tools.

Once you have taken inventory of your own swing, you know your baseline. Now, as an advanced golfer, you must develop a theory for how you can improve upon that baseline. Many professionals outsource this work to coaches, and you could probably pay a pro at your local course to do it for you. If you happen to belong to a club with an elite teaching professional, Harvey Penick, say, and you have the coin to outsource this work, go ahead. That said, I think if

---

79 Listen, I know that the feel in your hands is strictly subjective and not objective. The feeling you get at strike is more consistent and predictable, and so more trustworthy, than the feeling of your body in motion. There is a definite binary between a flush and a clank.

you develop your approach on your own, you will always have more ownership over your swing, which will help you keep improving. Another set of eyes is always handy when you get stuck, though. You don't have to do this all on your own.

Once you have a theory, the next step is to actually try to implement the change into your swing. As I've told you ad nauseam, your sense of proprioception is inadequate to change your swing by feel alone. So what do you do? You could try to randomly change things until something sticks, which is what I did as a kid. But that process is inefficient and not guaranteed to have any success. What I do now, and what I would recommend, is to prescribe yourself drills.

Throughout this book, I have highlighted some drills I like for specific swing issues.[80] The purpose of a drill is to give you some immediate feedback so that you can overcome the limits of your proprioception and mold your swing more closely to some ideal. Given your swing change theory, you could make up your own drill. You could also just use Google, though a lot of people have made these changes over the years. I think a good drill will have some hard feedback mechanism, which will always tell you when your move has gotten out of a certain tolerance range. I think a stick in the ground and a towel under the armpit are good tools. Your brain will try to trick you in training, but physical tools never will. Use these to develop or adapt drills. Just beware of Goodhart's law: any measure that becomes a target ceases to be a good measure. Work your drills. Don't let them work you.

---

80 Note that these drills are in no way comprehensive.

While you may not need a camera to train, it is a game changer. Use your precious range time to drill your drills and take videos to assess your progress. You should be able to see your actual swing transforming into your theoretical swing as you go.

One thing you should know is that when you start a swing change, the first thing that will happen is you're probably going to hit some terrible shots. You don't yet know how to use your new swing, and while you develop the technique, it will almost feel like you're going backward. That's why it is essential to develop and commit to a theory. If you overreact to your first range session with a new swing, you'll never make any progress. You have to give your swing change the time to be incorporated into your routine. You should assess your progress intermittently using all the tools I gave you—contact, flight, and video—and then take your swing change out on the course. But you should stick with your plan for enough time for it to be meaningful.

That said, you don't have to commit to it forever. Some swing changes are wrong. Look at what Hank Haney did to Tiger Woods! But you have to give it time. After a few weeks or a month, you should know on the golf course whether it's worked or not.

That's practice, baby! Assess your flaws, develop a theory, create a plan of action, work on your plan, and assess your progress. Rinse, repeat. The same method applies to putting and chipping as well.

I think it's important to remember to devote time to repeating the correct motions that you already know, especially in the context of putting and chipping. Your touch and feel depend on tiny unconscious refinement (which I think happens in your nervous system) and are better trained by repetition than by reworking your motion. That is not to say that the same flaw, theory, implementation, and assessment approach shouldn't be applied here. It just should maybe be less central to your approach. Develop a consistent putting and chipping stroke and then drill those down.

You should also always be playing actual golf regularly. While your practice sessions will help you develop particular constituent skills, the art of scoring will only come out on the course. If you just play competitive rounds every day, the odds are good that by the end of the year you will have improved dramatically. I think the practice sessions are important to maximizing your development, but don't let them come at the expense of playing real golf. That is the whole fucking point anyway.

SCORING PRACTICE

As an advanced golfer, much of the information informing your practice routine should come from the course. Being a better golfer does not mean being a better range player; it means scoring. You need to figure out which misses are costing you strokes and focus your practice time on those issues—in this way, you will get the highest return on investment.

Traditional notions of practice partitioning do not necessarily align with the areas where you stand to gain the most strokes on the golf course. When I was a kid, old-timers always told me not to practice hitting driver: "You only hit it six or seven times a round"; "You already hit it far." The reality was that I was hitting my drives out of bounds once or twice a round, and I was out of position another three or four times. This one club cost me five to ten strokes a round. I realized, far too late in life, that I wasn't even accurate with my driver on the range. The advice I had been getting, "Don't practice that too much," harmed my game. When I made driver the focus of my practice sessions, I saw improvements in my scoring in a month that persist to this day.

This might not be driver for you. Maybe you're shanking too many chips. Maybe you're leaving your putts short. Maybe you're just not that accurate with your wedges. Whatever it is, play golf, figure it out, and make a plan to improve.

Target your flaws ruthlessly, intentionally, one at a time, and your game will improve rapidly. This advice will never cease to be the most useful way to improve yourself, even when marginal gains become harder to come by. You can always identify what you're worst at and create a targeted plan to get better. If you self-evaluate readily, this shit will shoot you into the stratosphere.

There are other elements of scoring that you have to practice as well. I mentioned this in the scoring chapter, so I won't belabor the point. You have to get used to the ball going in the hole and get used to recovering from bad shots without losing your head. If you control your mind, you can control your ball, which is the key to good scoring.

CHAPTER 9

PLAYING GOLF

GOLF IS A GAME. IF IT ISN'T FUN, YOU'RE DOING IT WRONG. SURE, some of that fun comes from self-improvement and manifesting your goals. But some of it is from appreciating the world's natural beauty, walking in nature with your brothers and sisters, and heckling the shit out of friends and foes alike. Until now, this book's goal was to teach you a way to think about learning golf and give you some core knowledge to get started. But the game isn't just about mastering the skills; it's about *playing golf.* The next few sections focus on that pursuit.

THE RULES OF GOLF

The USGA publishes a book called *The Rules of Golf.* I highly recommend you pick it up! Most pro shops will give you a copy for free.

It will be mightily helpful in understanding the baroque system of traditions governing the game over here (if you're in the UK, you can refer to the R&A rules, which pertain over there). Knowing the rules is really handy because if you're playing in an official competition, you must adhere to them to the letter.[81] The same goes for club competition, with the caveat that clubs have local rules you also must respect (unless the rules include on-course out of bounds, in which case, as I mentioned, they can fuck right off).

You won't play most of your golf in competition, though. And you better understand the difference between a Sunday game and an official competition if you want anyone to invite you back to their weekend rounds. Growing up, I saw people grouse endlessly about trivial bullshit, like playing out of turn. These people, the saying goes, are "Playing Rules." We here in Brogs' Big Bubble™ don't play rules; we play golf.

That means the rules should be more relaxed when we play with the homies. To play a more relaxed, fun game of golf, you have to know which rules matter and can't be bent and what should be negotiated with your playing partners before the round.

I told you before that you can't move your ball, ever. That's rule number one. Play the ball as it lies. If you don't respect that rule,

---

81 Note that not one week after I wrote this section I saw Viktor Hovland and Joel Dahmen argue with Daniel Berger over a drop at the Players Championship in Jacksonville. Seeing these professionals passive-aggressively pout changed my opinion here. There is never a good reason to argue over drops. Nobody has the fucking patience. The correct response to a bad drop is side-eye, anything more will annoy me, even with $3.4 million on the line. Sorry.

you're not playing golf. You got a shit lie, tough beans. Everybody knows which players are improving their lies, identifies them as cheaters, and ridicules them for it. This game is not serious enough to cheat your friends over.

That being said, there are some exceptions to this! For instance, if you're playing a noncompetitive round with the homies, noncompetitive means there is no ongoing game. Feel free to fluff your lie, roll your ball, or whatever you want. In that case, I believe that you're just practicing, and you may safely use your discretion as to what's best for your game. Feel free even to keep score under these conditions, although you will know, and your partners will know, that your score is fake. As far as I'm concerned, feel free to upload that score onto the GHIN database for purposes of your handicap. In this case, you will be developing what we like to call a "vanity handicap," and the only person you will be cheating by doing that is yourself. Swing free, sailor.

Another key exception is *in* casual competition with your friends. Talk to your partners about the rules you will enforce in the round. If it's late or early in the season, or you're all not feeling it, play winter rules. That means that wherever your ball is, you can pick it up, clean it, and replace it somewhere near where it landed, without penalty. If the fairways are wet or muddy, play lift-clean-replace, basically the same thing. You and your partner can decide if rough is included in this or if it's fairway only. I think enforcing a close radius for these free drops is a waste of time, but don't be an asshole about it! These rules allow you to improve your lies, and you should use them to your advantage. But if you move your ball 10 yards closer to the hole, you're a loathsome snake. Tread that line carefully and respectfully, and you'll be fine.

These flexible rules can be applied after the start of a round too. If the conditions worsen or seem unfair during a round, change the rules you're playing under. A common area where this comes up is in bunkers on municipal golf courses (we call these "munis"), which aren't always maintained to the exacting standards we might prefer. If the bunkers suck, maybe you and your partners want to take a drop out of them. Fine by me, man; just discuss it.

More than this, you might find other unfair conditions out on the course, like ground under repair or casual water, where you may be entitled to a drop. Even here, where the rules say you can drop, ask your opponent. This is just a sportsmanship thing, and it will contribute to a culture of trust in your round. Your opponent should, of course, freely allow these drops without a second thought. If they don't, they're scum and don't play with them. But you still have to ask. If they happen to be far away, it's acceptable to take a drop unilaterally and then tell your opponent after, but that won't contribute as robustly to the culture of trust.

Drops come up relatively often, so remember that a drop is not the same as placing the ball. To take a drop, aim for a spot no farther than two club lengths from the spot of the ball (or the place it went into a hazard or water) and no closer to the hole and drop the

LET THE BIG DOG EAT

ball from knee height. It's important to respect these rules during competition.

In contrast to drops, which I think should be freely given, mulligans, in my opinion, have no place in the game. If you are unfamiliar, a mulligan is when you redo a shot without penalty. It is incredibly common for novice golfers to think it's acceptable after a bad shot to simply reload and whack it again. I *hate* this for a few core reasons. First, taking mulligans is a terrible practice strategy and will make you a worse golfer. Most players, particularly novice or intermediate players, hit the ball much better on the range than on the course. This is because they're unaccustomed to the pressure of playing with real stakes. When you give yourself a chance to reload and play the shot again, *even in practice*, I think you remove the psychological stakes that make golf difficult and give yourself no opportunity to practice real shotmaking with consequences.

This, to me, means that playing with mulligans, with any mulligans ever, is not golf. Golf is a game of hitting shots and accepting the consequences. Remove that element, allow yourself to skirt consequences, and you're not playing golf.

The other issue with reloading is that it's slow as hell, and this game is already tortuously slow. A healthy adult walking on an open course can play eighteen holes in around two hours; I know because I've done it many times. The rounds you are likely to play, on the other hand, will take four or five hours. That means that 50% of your time out there is just spent being delayed and waiting. Suppose you reload and hit shots over and over again. In that case, it just contributes to this grinding delay and will inevitably drive your partners crazy. Don't do it. Hit your shots, accept the consequences, and shut the fuck up. Move on.

I will make a slight exception for breakfast balls and mulligans that some players grant for the first shot on the first tee. The purpose of the breakfast ball is to allow for a gentle warm-up. Most muni tracks don't have driving ranges, and it's hard to hit the ball stiff. These are okay, I guess. I get the reasoning. We are all of us getting older, and this leaves us pretty stiff on the first tee. Most of these games are meant to be fun anyway. I still think breakfast balls are bullshit, to be quite honest. But if you need one for yourself, it's your shame, not mine.[82]

Other trivial rules, like playing in turn or tapping the ball by accident and causing it to move, should be liberally disregarded in casual play. Everyone occasionally makes their ball move a tiny bit by accident. It's not a big deal and shouldn't result in a penalty in your beer round. In official competitions, where all the rules should be respected to the letter, these fringe penalties should be enforced, but not in casual golf.

You can't ground your club in the bunker before your shot, and you should respect that rule. Don't rest the club down in the sand

---

82 If you happen to be a member at a private course, and you have the time and inclination, I think it's acceptable to go out at dusk when other players aren't using the course and hit five to ten shots from a particular spot. I think in particular this is useful for honing your approach shots. This is different than reloading in a round. If you do want to practice at dusk this way, feel free to ask forgiveness rather than permission from your local course. Just be mindful not to disrespect the course by cutting a big swath of divots in the fairway.

or carve an area for your shot. If you touch the sand by accident, though, it's not the end of the world, dude. We don't have to count that. Again, if you're playing with some sad Nazi who wants to hold all these against you, just don't play with them again.

This doesn't cover every rule, but you should have a feel for the standards I am setting. The goal is to set a loose approach where nobody cheats, but people feel comfortable. Golf is meant to be fun, and this approach preserves that. The key is communication with your partners about what is and isn't permissible and respecting the terms you agree on together.

UNWRITTEN RULES

Beyond rules, our competitions come with standards for how we treat each other. I just gave you one. Drops should be freely given unless the ask is egregious. Don't be miserly toward your opponents; everyone will have a good time. There are more like this, and they start on the green.

In match play, opponents have the choice to "give" their opponent putts, meaning that your opponent can pick the ball up and count the putt as made. This is useful to speed up play and generally makes casual golf more fun by removing some of the slippery short putts we all hate. In my view, though, no putt ever *must* be given. I have seen really good golfers get angry about this, and I thought that they were all in the wrong. If you're putting, you must actively get the signal from your opponent that a putt is given before you pick it up, and if they don't give it to you, tough beans. I have seen many golfers pick up balls as if they were good without their opponents signaling that the putt given. Doing this is forfeiting the hole. I'm sorry, bud; you don't get anything free unless your opponent gives it to you. It's totally acceptable to ask your opponent if a putt is good. You should do it every time you think it might be unless your opponent signals to you first. It ain't given if they don't give it to you, though.

In golf, the ball isn't in the hole until the ball is in the hole, and you should expect to have to putt out everything. I think the expectation that putts will be given makes some players worse short putters, always living in fear that their opponent will disarm them by making them face themselves alone out on the green.

So no putt is ever automatically given, but if you take that to mean that you should never give putts, then you're an asshole and we hate you. In real competition, this is fair. Jason Day played this strategy in the WGC Match Play tournament in Austin, and totally threw his opponent off. A little gamesmanship is well supported if millions of dollars are on the line. In your beer match, though, you should give all the putts you think your opponent is nearly certain to make. You don't *have* to, but again, if you don't, you're an asshole.

There are some general strategies around giving putts that you'll want to know in deciding when to give your opponents putts and when to hold back. First, I never give putts to lose a round or a side. If you're going to beat me, you have to beat me. If you think the putt is a guarantee, let's see it. This is just simple. I won't quit and concede a round, so I won't concede a putt that would end a round. You can quit your matches if you want, but I will think that you're soft if I hear about it. I've had people miss these putts and then complain. Who are you really mad at?

The second situation should be obvious, but don't give putts that are actually hard. Some very short putts still have break in them, and these slippery boys should be served to your opponents on the half shell. Don't save opponents from feeling their palms sweat.

Third, if your opponent is a bad short putter, you sadly must exploit them to punish their weakness so that they will learn to be big and strong like you. Until they make a shorty, you don't give them a shorty. And then, even once they do, you make them prove it a few times through the round. If they start missing again, they don't get any putts. Some people like to play this the other way and give bad short putters all their putts until one comes up that really counts, thinking that they won't be able to build confidence. I think the humiliation from missing these repeatedly is so crushing that it can start to bleed over into other parts of their game, and so I prefer to let them keep missing.

Other than these situations, though, you should be giving most putts within 3 feet. Some players will check the putts with their putter to see if they're in the zone, but remember, giving putts is a matter of your discretion. Their putter length doesn't mean jack shit.

Trash-talking on the golf course has its own informal rules and standards that you should be aware of. Golf gives an excellent canvas for all kinds of jibes and half manipulations. Harvey Penick said that the best one he ever heard was when a player on the tee asked his opponent if he "breathed in or out on his downswing." Harvey Penick also said that these were the domain of the mentally weak or afraid, but I disagree: I think they're fun, and I think they're part of the game.

Before you start talking shit, you should know what not to do. Do NOT lie to your opponent or try to convince them to hit a shot somewhere you know they will lose it. Quite the opposite, if you have a rangefinder or GPS software on your phone, you should freely let your opponent check it and give them truthful information. Golf is not a game of deception. We are brothers in this, and the game is hard enough as it is. You should never talk intentionally during your opponent's backswing unless it's inconsequential and done for humor. If you do this once, okay, it can be pretty funny. But if you actually fuck up your opponent, let them reload. Doing it more than once is annoying, so just don't.

Beyond those standards, though, it's fair game to burrow deep into your opponent's brain like some sort of Mississippi boll weevil. Goad them into taking riskier shots (this is different from lying about the risks of those shots). Ask them questions about their technique to get them out of their subconscious and make them overthink shots. Helpfully remind them of trouble in front of them so that they can avoid it! Of course, if it makes them think about it while they swing, that wouldn't harm your game. You get the idea. The point is to gently prod your opponent but to do so in good fun. If they are truly despondent, they need a helping hand, not a push. If they're beating you, though, use all the faculties available to you to settle the score. You should count on them doing the same to you.

As much as golf tolerates gentle chiding, it is a game played with mutual respect. Once a golf ball is on the green, draw a mental line between it and the hole. Your opponent's "line" is lava, and you should never step on it under any circumstances. Make sure to give this "line" a wide-enough berth that nobody can think you have stepped on it. If you don't know exactly where your opponent plans to putt the ball, make an exaggerated show of stepping over an area of the green roughly where you imagine they might. This will likely suffice to show your respect, even if it doesn't actually avoid their line in practice.

Another important sign of respect comes after the round. When a game is concluded, that is, on the hole where a match ends, take off your hat and shake your opponent's hand. Repeat this exercise on the 18th hole. It doesn't matter how angry you are at your opponent; you must always show them this respect. That is the code.

DRINKING ON THE GOLF COURSE

Drinking and golf have a sordid relationship. John Daly said he played his best golf drunk, and I believe him. He also tells stories about manipulating his opponents into thinking he was more drunk than he actually was to get the edge. I think drinking makes you worse at golf, but it can also be very fun. Some people play better after one or two drinks because nerves are a big factor in their play, but that's just one or two drinks. After that, I think there is a linear negative relationship between your quality of play and the amount of alcohol you consume. Are you going to have just one or two drinks? If the answer is no, drinking will probably make you worse at golf.

As long as your friends are drinking with you, you shouldn't have too much of a competitive disadvantage. People become intoxicated at different rates, though, so beware of the big boys.

When I drank, the first thing that went was my short game. Chipping and putting are simply much more difficult when your equilibrium falters. Next was my driver. I found myself wildly slapping the ball in random directions and then struggling to make contact at all. Finally, my irons, the most reliable part of my game, would start coming up thin or burying in the turf. By then, though, I probably didn't care much anymore.

If you are going to dip into the dark arts, I suggest drinking beer or diluted cocktails if you must. Anything too strong, like a martini, will fuck you up too fast and wreck your round. If you drink a beer every hole and a half or so over five hours, you will come out drunk but not truly get there until the end, so you won't be completely hopeless. Suppose you want to play this strategy, but still wreck your round. In that case, I suggest you shotgun on par 3s, par 5s, both par 3s and par 5s, or incorporate some type of shotgun stakes into your betting. This will ruin your afternoon convincingly.

LET THE BIG DOG EAT

Transfusions are reckless, but they do go down nicely. When I drank, I also found some success bringing plastic bottles of whiskey out on a cold autumn or winter round to stay warm. Play around with it.

A couple of final notes on intoxicants. A few friends tell me they have never played a round without drinking. Don't do this. This is a beautiful game, best played with your mind. Having fun with your friends is a part of it, but it's not all of it. If you never play a sober round, you're missing out on the richness of the sport. Once in a while, wait until after the round to drink, or, god forbid, don't drink at all. Take in the scenery. Savor your shots. One day, you will hit your last one.

As far as weed is concerned, it makes me absolutely useless in any amount. If you want to play golf well, weed is your enemy. That said, one of the best players I ever played with regularly, a club pro in Maine, used to make homemade weed brownies and bring them to the course to share. He always smoked me on the course too, so what do I know? Weed has also been productively added to many of my rounds in California, most notably in the morning at Penmar in Venice, which is the best muni course in the country. Those rounds weren't my most inspired golf, though.

Any other drug is choose your own adventure as far as I'm concerned. If you want to do cocaine on a golf course, you have bigger problems, friend, and all I have to offer is a helping hand whenever you choose to receive it.

GAMES

So now you know how to play golf; I know because I taught you. You also have a feel for the kind of casual rules we enforce when we play for fun. These will probably be most of your rounds. I gave you a sense of the social mores that golfers observe on the course and how to avoid annoying the people around you. But what games should you actually play?

When I say games, some of you might blanch. Having only seen golf on TV, you might assume golf is stroke play. Not so. Golf is the practice of hitting a little ball into a hole far away. Stroke play is a game. But there are other games too, and, in fact, many of them are much better suited for casual golf than stroke play. I'll walk you through a few, so you have a starting point when you go out to the course.

The game that I was first introduced to, and the game you're probably most familiar with through watching tournament golf, is stroke play. You add up all your strokes over a round, and the player with the lowest number of strokes wins. Stroke play makes for beautiful and tense tournament golf and is very good at identifying the best players in the world over 72 holes, but fuck stroke play. If you play stroke play in your casual game, every shot counts. Consequently, you are left agonizing over every shot, taking you away from the pure enjoyment of your rare luck in being out on a golf course with your brothers. This is miserable and should be avoided. More than that, if players are not tightly grouped, one player may fall far behind or get far ahead of the others quickly, ending the game after relatively few holes and with no drama. All of this sucks. Don't play stroke play.

The next game, which is also sometimes played at tournaments, is match play. Match play is a little bit better than stroke play, and I give you permission to play it. In match play, each hole counts for one, and players compete to win holes by having the lowest score on the hole. Player handicaps are added on a hole-by-hole basis, going from the most difficult hole on the course to the easiest, which helps less skilled players compete. Players win by winning the most holes over a round. Holes that are tied count for "no blood," meaning they do nothing. This game tends to create more drama and can lead to meaningful putts on every hole. While you have my permission to play match play if you want, you still shouldn't because similar, but better, games are available to you.

The first game that you should play is Nassau. Nassau is essentially match play, except instead of one match, the game is broken into three matches: one on the front, one on the back, and one over the whole eighteen. Traditionally, this is played with a dollar value. So in a $5 Nassau, the winner of the front would get $5, the winner of the back gets $5, and the winner of the overall gets $5. You could also say that the winner of two of these three matches wins the Nassau (note that it's impossible to win both sides but lose the overall). Nassau is just a better version of match play for casual play because it creates more drama and opportunities for meaningful play. The betting mechanic of pressing can add a further wrinkle to the Nassau. After a player loses a side or the overall, they may immediately "press," which creates a new match for the remainder of the holes left on the pressed match and has the effect of going double or nothing on that match. Further losses can be re-pressed, resulting in potentially very large exposure. This can also be played as "best ball" by breaking a foursome into two pairs and taking the best score from each team for each hole to determine the winner.

The next game that you should play is skins. Skins is essentially match play, except when holes are tied, they carry over or are "pushed." This game is especially good with three or more people because many holes will push, meaning the hole's value carries over into the next hole, creating extremely high-leverage holes where entire rounds can be won or lost. Usually, each hole in a skins match will have a dollar value. For example, in a one-dollar skins match, each hole would be worth one dollar. So if you beat your opponent on all eighteen holes, they would owe you eighteen dollars. Note that while this game can be fun with two people, like sex, it's even better in threesomes or foursomes. The competitiveness of skins matches with two people can be dampened if someone plays better than their competitor, as they are likely to break open a big lead. My general guidance is to play Nassau when you have two people and skins when you have three or four.

If you have three people, another popular game is the nine-point game. The nine-point game kinda sucks for reasons I have never been able to perfectly articulate, but it's fine when you have three people and are tired of skins. In the nine-point game, each hole is worth nine points, and those points are distributed in the order the players finished the hole, first place gets five points, second place gets three points, and last place gets one point. If there are ties, you add up the points for the players who tied and divide them evenly between them. So, for example, if first and second tied, their eight points would be divided to give each player four points. If all three players tie, they all get three points. This game doesn't build any drama; it's just a game. Whatever. It's basically stroke play with more difficult-to-track scoring. Play it if you want.

If you have four people, though, you can play two other very fun games. One is modified best ball, playing six-hole matches. In this game, you play six-hole matches between the best-ball pairs, and after each match, you switch partners. This way, after eighteen holes, you will have had every other player as a teammate for six holes, making this game eminently fair.[83] Each match creates a net score of the match. For instance, players A and B won two up, which both players individually carry the net of throughout the round. Then in the next six-hole match, players A and C win one up, so now player A has three points, player B has two points, player C has one point, and player D has zero points. You add all the points to determine who won overall. You can choose to play ties as no blood or pushes. You can also play with "junk" or "dots." These are points added to your score in any game based on achieving certain things. In my most recent game, we gave dots for making a natural par[84] from the sand

---

83 Sometimes, admittedly, because of the way stroke holes are distributed across a course, it may not be fair. Whatever. Who cares.

84 "Natural" here means a par without strokes subtracted from a player's handicap.

(sandies), from the water (soggies), after hitting a tree (woodies), and after hitting the cart path (carties), as well as for natural birdies, net eagles, net albatross, and for hitting it closest to the pin on par 3s.

The final game I will teach you is called "wolf." It's fun once in a while but really toes the line of what I would consider "golf." I also think wolf outcomes are a little too arbitrary to be played frequently.

In wolf, you start the round by throwing balls[85] to determine a tee order. That order is maintained throughout the game and rotates each hole. So the player who went first on the first hole then goes last on the second hole, second to last on the third hole, second on the fourth hole, and first again on the fifth hole. After the cycle repeats four times, on the 17th and 18th holes, whichever player is DFL (dead fucking last) goes first, and the other players follow them in the original tee order. The player going first on each hole is the wolf, who has to choose teams. This means players can choose one of the other three as their teammate for the hole.

The teams compete in best ball in each hole. The wolf may choose at any time before picking teams to go "lone wolf," which will create two teams, one of the wolf and one of the other three players, and will also multiply the bet based on when it is chosen. The bet is quadrupled if the wolf calls a lone wolf on the tee before hitting a shot. It's tripled if they call it on the tee after hitting a shot. And

---

85 To "throw balls" one player collects a golf ball from each participant and throws them in the air. The player whose ball lands closest to the thrower goes first, next closest second, and so on.

if they call it after another player has hit a shot, the bet is doubled. These bets push and stack, so if I call lone wolf before I tee off on one, that quadruples the bet. If I push with my opponents, that means the next hole is worth five, and if player B, now the wolf, goes lone wolf after teeing off, the bet on the second hole is worth fifteen. This can get a little wonky, but it's not too complicated.

If the wolf doesn't go lone wolf, they must choose a teammate from one of the other players. The wolf can choose a player only between the time that player hits and the time the next player hits. If the wolf doesn't choose a player until the end of teeing off, the wolf may only choose between going lone wolf, doubling the bet, and selecting the last player to tee off. When the wolf chooses a teammate, the bet is not multiplied. There is a complex strategy to succeeding at wolf, but I don't like to share it lest my friends start beating me.

Of course, there are many other games in addition to these that I've described. But suppose you learn these and play them with your friends. In that case, you will have a very good start and be able to comfortably take charge in muni and country club situations alike.

EQUIPMENT

Now I have taught you much of what I think about the game, and I think it will also help you to know my thoughts on golf equipment. You can't play golf without clubs, so if you're going to be thoughtful about the game, you might as well be thoughtful here too.

When I was younger, I thought equipment didn't matter at all. I never had any money, but I was lucky to get a nice set of Ping i3+ irons from my dad and generally had pretty solid hand-me-down equipment. It was a little old, but I always thought it did the job. My philosophy then was that you play the game with your body, and a good player can do it with whatever equipment is available.

There may be some truth to this. Blaming equipment is a great way to excuse yourself from the many errors that we both know you are making. But as I've been able to replace my clubs, I realized my original tough-guy stance was actually just plain dumb.

Clubs matter a lot. You need clubs that fit you to play your best golf. I learned this way too late in life when I replaced those old Pings with new Ping blades with extra-stiff shafts. Playing with shafts that were too soft for me had for years given me a high, weak ball flight. The new clubs fixed that instantly. I had always thought that it was my fault, that I could just correct it with my swing, and maybe I could have, but sadly, I had been playing with the wrong clubs.

Don't make the same mistake I made. Get fitted. Get clubs that are right for your swing speed and skill level. I play blades because I usually hit the ball on the center of the clubface, and I think they give me the best control. I am aware that many people think this is dumb, and they may be right, but I like blades, and I'm confident with them.

You may find other factors that guide your choice of clubs. Generally, the larger and more cavity-backed the club, the more forgiving it will be and the farther and higher it will hit the ball. Use this to guide your choice based on what you need. I hit the ball plenty far but too high, so clubs with less cavity really helped me.

This is not to say that you need to replace your clubs often. I really think you don't. Once you have clubs that fit you, unless they break, there's not much reason to replace them except in a few discrete cases. First, drivers seem to get about 10 yards better every five years or so. If you don't replace them in that time frame, you're giving up some distance to your opponents.

I also think that the graphite shafts they put in drivers get a little weird after a few years of use, so you should replace those anyway. Second, grooves on wedges wear out and will spin the ball less with age and use. This is bad. Clean your grooves, get them sharpened (as long as this doesn't make them illegal), and replace your wedges a little more frequently than other clubs. That's it. Other than that, just play with the set that fits you, and as long as they don't break, there's no real need to update them.

Historically, my philosophy on equipment extended to putters as well. It is just a flat stick, I thought. How could it make any difference? I still don't really know how putter selection makes a difference, but I know that it does. Take that into consideration too. Try out a lot of putters and use the one you like. If you're struggling, I give you permission to change putters for no reason except to give your brain a reset and get you out of a rut.

Ultimately, you're a fool if you focus on equipment too much. Golf is for playing, and the equipment is just a tool to make it happen. If all you can play with are old spare women's clubs from the 1980s, as has been the case for me from time to time, you are still blessed to be on a golf course at all that day. This peace and prosperity we still enjoy in the twenty-first century is just a fleeting moment in the crush of history. Don't ignore equipment completely, however. It does matter. You'll play better with equipment that fits you, so, if you can, spend the time and money to get it right.

CHAPTER 10

THE END

Starting out in golf, I fixated on the great ball-strikers. Tiger Woods, Ben Hogan, even Moe Norman. I wanted to be like them, and so I made it my goal to completely control my ball in the air. I am nothing like those guys, though, and pursuing this goal caused me endless grief. My temperament, my talent, has never been for sustained precision.

In those early days, I put myself in a position where I was bound to be frustrated playing the game. I spent endless hours at the range trying to achieve perfection. When I actually played golf and I couldn't live up to that standard, all I wanted to do was scream. I almost quit, and I would just go out in the evenings and walk the course alone, enjoying the peace of being in the fresh air of a beautiful place.

As I grew and stopped focusing on competitive golf, I developed more admiration for fun-loving golfers with fluid swings. Freddie Couples was the icon. Bubba Watson tried to be that guy but never convinced anyone that he was much fun. Cam Smith and Louis Oosthuizen made a better impression.

There is perfection to being in sync with yourself on the golf course, even when the game doesn't go your way. I have always admired these golfers for teaching me something about that. None of their games were modeled on consistency or perfect ball-striking the way Hogan's was. Instead their swings are built on feel. Feeling the ball to the hole is very different from the militant precision I was trying to practice, and when I started to play like that, it gave me a lot of joy back.

The short game caught short shrift from me for a long time. As I was learning, my approach to chipping and putting was sometimes errant and, at times, dismissive. Growing up, I was always searching for the flashy home run ball. I tried to hit Phil's flop until I knew I could pop the ball up in the air. After that, I played every chip as a flop for a while. That was really dumb. In the early days of YouTube I scrounged for old videos of Seve Ballesteros and dreamed of emulating his brilliance. Tiger's artistry here should be mentioned as well.

I learned too late that the short game could really save you. That special touch and feel around the greens, the touch that only some people have, will give you an edge that's hard to match. A player with a dangerous short game is never out of a hole. The guy who is striking the ball beautifully and can't get it down, on the other hand, will look like a dunce.

I've come to admire Kevin Kisner and Jordan Spieth. You look at their games and wonder what they're good at. They don't hit the ball very far, or in Jordan's case, even very straight. They do all sorts of ugly things around the course. But at the end of the day, they get the ball down in fewer strokes than their competitors. Again and again, they perform. What are they good at? They're good at golf. That's the skill that now thirty-something Aaron is envious of.

I spent many years trying to hit the ball hard, shape it in all kinds of interesting ways, hit flop shots, and impress my friends. But really, those things don't matter. Competing is getting the ball down. It took me a long time to learn that.

Those other things are fun, though.

I called this book *Let the Big Dog Eat* because I want to express an ethos. Golf is silly, but it's beautiful, communal, and rewarding too. I think if you like it and want to play golf, it is worth taking seriously and investing time, thought, and effort in it. This book is an attempt to jump-start that process by seeding you with my knowledge.

But golf remains silly, and I want readers of this book to remember that and bake it into their expectations. You can't take it *too* seriously. The right way to play golf is relaxed in the knowledge that you're very lucky to be where you are. Living in the moment, out in the vast fields of green, and in the company of your brothers and sisters.

The End

Some of the best experiences on the golf course aren't victories or successes but simple instances of peace and comfort. I remember practicing at Purpoodock in the evenings, and the sound of the little peeping frogs native to southern Maine. I remember whiskey at twilight on Bethpage Black. I remember a two-hour round in the rain in Savannah. These moments of serenity are worth playing for.

Golf is not that important, but the lessons you learn on a golf course can be life lessons. I won't be the first person to tell you that life is hard and will beat you down if you let it. In my view, the tools that I've learned through golf are the tools that we all need in life to make the most of our precious time.

In practice, I advocate for careful study, recordkeeping, and intentionality. It takes faith to face the unknown and build a new swing. To improve, you have to be willing to risk losing some of what we have already built. These skills, I think, serve us well in any pursuit we take up along this road.

I advocate mindfulness in competition. This practice helps build the resiliency to stick to a plan under pressure. You have to be able to face up to doubts and negativity. The truth is, just as we are certain to hit bad shots on the golf course, we are certain to make mistakes off the course. As we age, we are certain to watch as everything we love withers and dies. Careful mindfulness and studied resiliency are the best tools to face that certain fate with the grace to keep moving forward.

I suggest that you allow humor and joy in your golf game. Cherish each moment. Someday, we will all take our last swing and have no legacy to show for it. In the face of this horror, gratitude is the only practice that makes sense.

There is truth in self-improvement and actualization, but the fun is part of it too. Sometimes you just have to stand up to the tee on a par 5, take a nice wide stance, tee it high, and swing as hard as you can. Sure, you might lose a few balls, but you'll pipe a few bombs too.

Achieving one thing well, putting into practice one good habit, can be the source of many good habits and many things done well down the line. We own our swings. As life takes things away from us, we will always be able to return to the golf course for something of our own. Our bodies will deteriorate, and with them some of our skill, but we will always be able to find new aspects of golf to practice and refine. I find a sense of security in knowing that will always be an outlet for me here.

I developed these lessons over years of trial and error, teaching myself how to be the best I could with the resources available to me at any given time. I hope that you will use them judiciously and pass them on. The game will outlive us, and our traditions will survive us. From the moment you take a club in your hand, you contribute to that. Enjoy it.

The End

ACKNOWLEDGMENTS

WHEN I STARTED WRITING THIS BOOK IN 2022, I DIDN'T THINK anyone would ever read it. Now I know that at least twelve people have, which feels like a great triumph.

I initially self-published *Let the Big Dog Eat*, garnering roughly, oh, zero attention from the public. It came to be published by VeloPress through a quite fortuitous series of events that I want to document here.

In January of 2023 my friend Danielle Falls invited me to come to an event called "PatchinKucha VII." The host, Julie Picquet, encountered the Japanese narrative format "PechaKucha" somewhere in her travels. In a PechaKucha, a speaker creates a deck of twenty slides, and displays each for twenty seconds, to create a short, punchy, presentation.

Julie adapted it to the downtown professional scene in New York and solicited presenters from her friends. At PatchinKucha VII, for example, I learned about Fire Island's "Meat Rack" and the economics of counterfeit merchandise sold on Canal Street in New York.

Somehow I missed the invites for PatchinKuchas VIII and IX, but on July 17, 2023, I received an invitation to PatchinKucha X. I had released *Let the Big Dog Eat* on Amazon in June but had no idea how to find any readership. I knew that I needed a publisher, marketing advice, or *something*. Who better than a room full of Big Tech hotshots for an impromptu brainstorming session, I thought.

I asked Julie if I could present, and despite having met me only twice, she very graciously told me I could. The event was scheduled on the evening of July 31.

I had a problem though: for my thirty-first birthday I had planned to hike Mount Katahdin in Maine with my high school friends Ian Black and Matt Cartmell. We were going up on the 30th. Climbing Katahdin is a rite of passage in Maine. It's four hours of mostly bad road north of Portland, and parking permits are hard to come by. I had never climbed it and I wasn't going to cancel.

We woke up before sunrise on the 30th and hiked seven hours up and down. The path took us up over vast boulder fields and peaked at the "Knifes Edge," a rocky traverse with thousand-foot drops on either side. The climb was spectacular, but by the time I got back to my parents' house in Cape Elizabeth I was dead tired. I wasn't presenting the next day till 7:30 p.m., but it's a six-hour drive to Manhattan.

I planned to leave early on the 31st, but I was too dead to go in the morning. I pushed it to the last minute I could, in such visible pain while packing that my mom begged me not to go. I had my motorcycle with me in Maine and had to take it back to the city too. I just couldn't see any way around it. As I tied down my yellow North Face duffel, I knew she was right. I started to feel a grim unease, but I had to go. Making my way to the highway, an F-350 came fast around a corner and forced me off the road, laying on the horn as he screamed past. A bad omen.

Mostly I kept my head down as I plodded down the northeast. Around Hartford a car honked and I instinctively bristled, the F-350 still on my mind. On the highway you have to make your own space. Too vulnerable on the bike to give ground. Every few minutes I checked that I was still making time. Had to get there by 7:30. A few minutes late but I'd make it. In my head I was rehearsing what I'd say at the PatchinKucha. This might be my only chance to publish this book.

Around Bridgeport, another car honked. I looked back but my helmet blocked the view in my periphery. I didn't see what the matter was and was too focused on getting to New York to give it much pause. Then I felt something shift behind me.

I turned quickly to see the bungee cords holding my bag down on fire and feel the duffel fly off the back of the bike. On some bump the bag had slipped over the bike's high scrambler pipes and started to heat up with exhaust.

Acknowledgments

I pulled over to the side of the highway and saw my bag sitting five hundred feet back in traffic. This is the northeast corridor of I-95—probably the busiest road in the United States. I didn't know how I was going to get it. As soon as I started to turn, though, a stranger stopped his car with hazards on and grabbed it. He handed it to me and just as quickly drove away. Never underestimate the kindness of strangers.

I had to assess my situation. I was still two hours from New York, my bag had large holes where it had caught fire, and my bungies were gone. I checked the map and realized there was a Home Depot a few miles up, but with no way to secure my duffel to the bike I didn't have any idea how I'd get there. I called my insurance company's roadside assistance hotline, and they offered exactly jack shit. At this point, I nearly gave up hope. I emailed Julie: "I ran into some bike trouble and got delayed. So I think I will be almost an hour late."

Suddenly, out of nowhere, a tow trucked pulled in front of me and a man shouted, "Need some help?" "Can you take my bag to Home Depot?" I said. "What?" "To Home Depot, just up the road." I gave him the address and he said "Okay," looking bemused.

We got to the parking lot a few minutes later. He gave me my bag and drove off. Never asked for money or anything. Never underestimate the kindness of strangers.

I assessed my situation. I hadn't eaten since the morning and could feel myself physically shaking. Highway time exacts a toll, and the shoulder is even worse. In Home Depot I bought duct tape to patch the holes in my bag, new bungies, and one Baby Ruth candy bar. I emailed Julie: "actually, more like 8:45."

I rolled into the city at 8:50, very much worse for wear, carrying my ruined bag with me to Julie's stoop. One ring. Nothing. Two. More silence. I knew they were downstairs already presenting and was just about to write an email when the door opened.

Of course I was the last one there, and when my presentation began, I really didn't have much to say anyway. It's just a silly golf book, after all. "I'm Aaron. This presentation is called: 'Buy My Book.'"

And of course everyone was lovely. They helped me brainstorm marketing ideas and talked about their friends who were authors and their experiences. They were more supportive than I ever hoped, considering not one knew me at all and I had just shown up weather-beaten and late. Some of them even bought my book.

Then we left. Julie sent me a nice email thanking me, and I counted my blessings that anyone would want to read some nonsense a stranger wrote about golf. From there I figured nothing more would come.

But a few days later, on August 3, Colleen McGinn, a fellow motorcyclist whom I had never met outside PatchinKucha, wrote me and cc'd her friend Bonnie Miller, a published author. I emailed Bonnie, whom I had never met at all, "I would love to know more about your experience."

Months went by, but no response. In the interim I traveled, sold a few more books, and generally bummed around. I figured if I ever wrote another book, that one would get published. This was just practice.

Then on October 31, Bonnie wrote me back. "I'm actually in NYC for a few more days this week if you're interested in a coffee chat!" We met a few days later, and she told me that she felt she had actually gotten lucky because one of her friends worked at a publisher. Despite not knowing me and not having read my book, she promised to put me in touch. I sent her a copy afterward, feeling very lucky myself.

On November 8, Bonnie wrote Casie Vogel at Ulysses Press, saying that she was impressed with *Let the Big Dog Eat* and recommending a meeting. A few hours later, Casie wrote that Ulysses had just acquired a sports publisher, VeloPress. Despite not having met me or read my book, she offered to put me in touch. The next day she connected me to Kierra Sondereker, who asked me to send a copy of the book and agreed to meet me.

On February 8, 2024, Kierra conveyed an offer to publish *Let the Big Dog Eat* with VeloPress. A full six months after I made the PatchinKucha presentation.

I wish I remember why I started writing this book. I remember vaguely wanting to find some creative outlet in my life, but the exact moment I started is lost to time. I checked my notes around the time and found this:

February 11, 2022
Principle:
Something not written down is lost.
If you have a question, ask someone for help.

Now having heard my story, you will see why I feel very fortunate that VeloPress is publishing this book. I never had any other offer to publish the book. Never had any other lead. If one thing went differently in that long string of chance, it never would have happened. So now that publication is imminent, I wanted to use this moment to write down the story before it's lost.

I'd also like to thank everyone along the way.

Thank you Danielle and Julie and Colleen and Bonnie and Casie and Kierra. Thank you to the two strangers who helped me on I-95 in Connecticut on July 31, 2023. Thanks again to my mom for looking out for me—I know that motorcycle ride really scared you. And thanks to everyone who ever reads this book. It's an incredible privilege for anyone to take an interest in something I wrote. I know it probably won't be many people, but like Pete Townshend said, "Just a little is enough."

ABOUT THE AUTHOR

AARON BROGAN IS A LAWYER BASED IN NEW YORK. EVEN YEARS after leaving his home in Maine, Brogan still enjoys fresh air, mountains, and the sea. When he's not in the courtroom or the golf course, he can be found traveling the world, attempting to distract himself from his inevitable death.